new crosswords 2

pocket posh® new crosswords 2

copyright © 2019 by Andrews McMeel Publishing.
All rights reserved. Puzzles copyright © 2019 by Andrews
McMeel Syndication. Printed in China. No part of this book may
be used or reproduced in any manner whatsoever without written
permission except in the case of reprints in the context of reviews.

Andrews McMeel Publishing
a division of Andrews McMeel Universal
1130 Walnut Street, Kansas City, Missouri 64106

www.andrewsmcmeel.com

19 20 21 22 23 RLP 10 9 8 7 6 5 4 3 2 1

ISBN: 978-1-5248-5334-1

Illustration by supermimicry/Getty Images

ATTENTION: SCHOOLS AND BUSINESSES
Andrews McMeel books are available at quantity discounts with
bulk purchase for educational, business, or sales promotional use.
For information, please e-mail the Andrews McMeel Publishing
Special Sales Department: specialsales@amuniversal.com.

new crosswords 2

Andrews McMeel
PUBLISHING®

THIS PUZZLE IS TABOO · By Claude Remmey

ACROSS

1 Reduce, as prices
6 Legendary hurdler Moses
11 Emeril Lagasse shout
14 Trunk in one's trunk
15 Pageant topper
16 "Star Wars" prologue word
17 No-no mediocre?
19 Like a sizzling fuse
20 Beach cooler
21 Prefix with "graphy"
23 Heineken, e.g.
24 Conviction
25 They stand on their own two feet
28 Fort Seward city
30 "Diary of ___ Housewife" (1970 film)
31 Bad thing to wreak
32 Sporty chapeau
35 Compass point 180 degrees from NNE
36 No-no no, slangily
38 U.N. worker protection grp.
39 ___ of a gun
40 FDA pt.
41 Ugly pond film
42 Some British noblemen
44 Sudden contractions
46 "The War of the ___"
48 "Where have you ___?"
49 They're a laugh a minute
50 Risk or Monopoly
55 Sort or kind
56 No-no free-for-all?

58 Peg with a concave top
59 Alaskan native
60 Type of rechargeable battery (Abbr.)
61 Commit a faux pas
62 Parts of hammer heads
63 Palatable

DOWN

1 Is no longer one of the firm?
2 Anecdotal wisdom
3 Side squared, for squares
4 What Brutus did to Caesar
5 It's more than dislike
6 Upper regions of space
7 Cameron of film
8 Have an eye-opening experience?
9 Anger
10 Event of being born
11 Science of flight dynamics
12 Gracefully athletic
13 Dominant theme
18 Visualizes
22 Some schooner cargo
24 Short personal histories
25 Opposite of treble
26 The Pointer Sisters's "___ Excited"
27 One making loans
28 Returnees from Mecca
29 Classic door-to-door cosmetics marketer
31 "The Battle ___ of the Republic"
33 Homecoming attendee, briefly

34 Some soccer game observers

36 Custody

37 Big commotions

41 Fruit-filled wine beverage

43 Key below Z, on PCs

44 Some Bosnians

45 Intellectual nitpicker

46 Order to someone moving away

47 Fuel-carrying vessel

48 Matting fibers

50 Color of suede shoes of song

51 Thor's father

52 Pendulum paths

53 "One man's ___ is another man's poison"

54 Circular current

57 End of lunch time, maybe

2 · YOUR TURN AT BAT · By Gary Cooper

ACROSS

1 What subwoofers supply
5 "Is this your idea of ___?" ("I'm not amused")
10 From square one
14 One of the five Olympic rings
15 Shunned colony resident of yore
16 French family member
17 Babe Ruth's nickname
20 Certain metalworkers
21 Fleur-de-___ (symbol on Quebec's flag)
22 Bard's nightfall
23 Anti-drug ad, e.g.
24 Pass ___ (make the grade)
27 Sideless cart
29 Jack of nursery rhymes
32 Not nay
33 Endless years
36 How trapeze artists perform
38 What a baseball player's life is full of?
41 One who pays
42 Vowelless degree
43 A founder of Dadaism
44 Doles (out)
46 Loud cry of pain
50 Southfork locale on TV
52 Unneeded command for chowhounds
55 Onassis's X
56 Boathouse wall hanging
57 Moved by degrees in one direction only

60 Start conducting
63 Pitcher with a wide spout
64 Extra-strong cotton thread
65 ___ and for all
66 Have a restless night
67 Genuflection joints
68 More than merely want

DOWN

1 RBI word
2 Paler
3 Earth pigment
4 Impudent back talk
5 "... calm, ___ bright"
6 Some VWs
7 Silvery fish
8 Burns and Berry
9 Leandro's love
10 Point in orbit
11 Scoop for a fashion magazine
12 Time for the history books
13 Rain-soaked
18 One who cries foul?
19 Ian Anderson or James Galway
24 Comic Cheech
25 Squirmy catches
26 2004 biopic nominated for Best Picture
28 Himalayan humanoid
30 Military chaplain
31 Stage of sleep, for short
34 East German currency
35 NBA legends Archibald and Thurmond

37 Like a burnt-out briquette
38 Zeus's spouse
39 Says "please" and then some
40 Volleyball obstacle
41 X-ray unit
45 Reach an agreement out of court
47 87 or 91 at the pump
48 From what source
49 Covered, as Tupperware

51 Lions' dens
53 Nagging pains
54 Word in many band names
57 Completely botch
58 Cathedral feature
59 Black, in a sonnet
60 Workplace for an actor
61 Pencil number
62 Yellowstone bugling beast

5

3 | JAM SESSION · By Phil Kaufman

ACROSS

1 Sign before Virgo
4 Spa feature
9 ___-win situation
13 Thole mates?
15 Respond to, as advice
16 "Do ___ others as ..."
17 Hit video game series since 2005
19 Chimney passage
20 More crafty
21 Communion bread holder
23 "... a grin without a cat!" thinker
25 Some Italians
28 Witch's laugh
30 Bad-hair-day helper
31 Salesman, informally
32 Duke Ellington's "Take ___ Train"
33 Exercise walk site
36 Easy to reach
38 Some rock concert highlights
41 A bit more than a walk-on
44 "Hey, what's the big ___?"
45 Unit of perspiration
49 "Starpeace" performer Yoko
50 Vase with a pedestal
52 Deals from the bottom
54 Most stuck-up
58 Yachtsman's neckwear
59 Unfasten, in a way
60 Toasters may drink to yours
62 Clay cooking pot
63 Heroic seaman Horatio
67 Alternative to Aspen
68 This, this, and this
69 Era-spanning story
70 ___ and sciences
71 Planted seeds
72 Hither and ___

DOWN

1 Ship's daily record
2 ___ Claire, Wisc.
3 Hole in the head?
4 Bangalore wrap
5 Aerobics aftereffects
6 Wombs
7 " ___ any drop to drink"
8 Defective vision
9 Civilian clothes, for a soldier
10 Get out of the habit of
11 Dazed or amazed
12 It may have a painted nail
14 Military jail
18 "Beverly Hills Cop" character Foley
22 Clipped conjunction
23 One fifth of "Hamlet"
24 "Well ___-di-dah"
26 Daphnis's love
27 Espionage figure
29 Aussie trotter
34 Ammonia compound
35 It's dropped for a trip
37 Danger in old homes
39 Paperboy's itinerary
40 Anita Brookner novel, "Hotel du ___"

6

41 ___ lettuce (romaine)
42 Forming a ring
43 Like a romantic night
46 How kids are told to look when approaching traffic
47 From ___ Z
48 When to spring forward (Abbr.)
51 Some are civil
53 School monitor's beat

55 Autumn stones
56 "The Taming of the ___"
57 Drama-filled
61 All tucked in
62 Biological eggs
64 "Eureka!" relative
65 Psych 101 topic
66 Went lickety-split

7

HANG AROUND · By Andy Tennison

ACROSS

1 Summoned, as the butler
5 Gun or ear cleaner
9 M.D.'s milieus
14 Dish of many ingredients
15 Simple test answer
16 Fiber-___ cable
17 Prison yard residents
18 Itty-bitty bit
19 Populous Japanese city
20 Parting words for someone moving away
23 Cash in Ginza
24 Jumping-off place
25 Bother persistently
27 Fine cotton thread
30 Hayseed TV series
32 "___ You Smarter Than a 5th Grader?"
33 Fill with bubbles
36 Completely closed
39 Participate in a primary
41 Tennis star Williams
42 Word of contempt
43 Pay to play
44 Formed whirlpools
46 Shepherd's expanse
47 Gauchos' plains
49 Nonreactive, as some gases
51 Reaches its highest level
53 Not crazy
55 Young kiltie
56 Be steadfast
62 Pueblo material
64 Great Lake port
65 Furnace film
66 Mr. Bean portrayer Atkinson
67 Benefit event, often
68 "You, Me and Dupree" actor Wilson
69 Magnani and Christie
70 Remaining to be paid
71 Travel agency to the stars?

DOWN

1 Music genre
2 Skin-cream additive
3 September's number
4 Another music genre
5 Con that cons a con man
6 Emulated Anne Rice
7 Coupe or sedan
8 Priority male?
9 Commotion
10 Photo ___ (pol's news events)
11 "Don't go yet"
12 ___ Peak, Colo.
13 Tasks at checkout counters
21 Invention inspiration
22 Word that always brings a smile?
26 Carpenter's file
27 Source of pumice
28 Item in many hotel room closets
29 "Cool it!"
30 They travel around the clock
31 Place for embroidery scissors
34 "Despite that ..."
35 Upgrade, as the decor

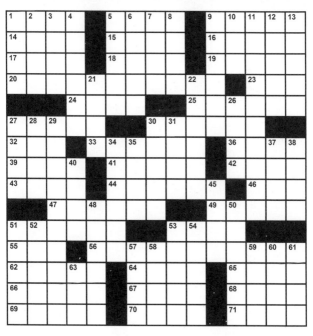

37 ___-friendly (easy to operate)
38 Yonder thingamabob
40 Snaky creatures
45 Wine partner
48 Georgia city
50 Singer Willie
51 Bow, the "It Girl"
52 Invisible health hazard
53 Metro-station entrance

54 Winning, for now
57 Brand of building blocks
58 Tournament seeding
59 The Hawkeye State
60 Column of boxes on a
   questionnaire
61 Destructive volcano in Sicily
63 Ovine oration

ACROSS

1 Garage occupant
5 Secure, as a nautical rope
10 Merganser relative
14 Mushroom
15 Opposite of oafish
16 "I Know Why the Caged Bird Sings" author Angelou
17 An unbelievable tale
20 A-teams, in high school
21 "___ be a pleasure"
22 Chicago-to-Detroit dir.
23 Long-eared beast of burden
24 Shakespearean king of the fairies
27 Certain Bosnian
29 Chop into tiny bits
32 Atty's assn.
33 Nineteenth-century presidential nickname
36 Leather source
38 Something of trivial importance
41 Death Valley is below it
42 Former U.S. capital
43 Play a role
44 Organization for high IQ folk
46 Racing vehicle
50 "Oy, vey!" cause (Var.)
52 Tricycle rider
55 ___-wee Herman
56 Thing, in law
57 Early inhabitant
60 Beautifully clear, as a complexion
63 Totally enjoying
64 Clear, as a frozen windshield
65 Wile E. Coyote's favorite brand
66 Garden of Genesis
67 "They Died With Their Boots On," e.g.
68 College aid consideration

DOWN

1 Tequila sources
2 Cosmopolitan
3 Musician on the road
4 Has the legal title to
5 Thai monetary units
6 Self-centeredness
7 Severe sentence
8 Clerical vestments
9 Pro vote
10 Whacked, old-style
11 Comic-strip magician
12 Potato protuberance
13 "The ___ We Were" (1973 movie)
18 World Factbook org.
19 Bell of note
24 Arctic, for one
25 Geishas' sashes
26 Staple of Indian cuisine
28 Fertility god
30 Adored ones
31 Aerialist's safeguard
34 Complexion spoiler
35 North Pole artisans
37 It's often around a foot?
38 Min. fractions

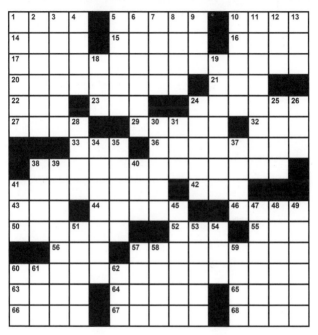

39 Develop and ripen
40 Pork place
41 Had a seat
45 This instant
47 For each thing
48 Supply with a new title
49 Came down cats and dogs
51 Short exploratory mission
53 "___ in the court!"

54 Recurrent twitch
57 On open waters
58 Sole tempter
59 The "G" in GTO
60 Epitome of easiness
61 Draw to a close
62 Tokyo, formerly

PLANT YOURSELF DOWN · By Cameron Rooney

ACROSS

1 Bottom line in fashion
4 Full nelsons, e.g.
9 With the bow, in music
13 ___ League (Middle Eastern alliance)
15 Man-___-town
16 Low river dam
17 Shy person at a social event
19 Destiny
20 Linger aimlessly
21 Sight organs
23 Chews like a beaver
25 Stand for
28 Oliver, Jay, and Sheree
30 "___ out!" (ump's cry)
31 Sticky hair product
32 A language of Pakistan
33 Sailor's stopover
36 Mary Poppins was one
38 Expand
41 Cowboy competition
44 Window part
45 A device for catching animals
49 Greek H
50 "The Simpsons" grandpa
52 Holmes or Poirot
54 Alloy's principal component
58 Placed on Capri
59 ___ apso (small terrier)
60 Become wider, as pupils
62 Teamwork wreckers
63 Of the common people
67 "___ every voice and sing ..."
68 Led Zeppelin's "Whole ___ Love"
69 "Shoulda, woulda, coulda" one
70 Dull-witted ones
71 Cast off from the body
72 Mai ___ (rum cocktail)

DOWN

1 End of a bray
2 The Roaring Twenties, e.g.
3 Wild dabbling duck
4 "Hold it right there!"
5 Orchestra tuners
6 English novelist Malcolm
7 Expected to arrive
8 Disco light
9 Dreadful
10 Change the order of
11 Watch brand
12 Metal on its way to a refinery
14 Dart shooter
18 Pike or perch
22 Horn-shaped object
23 Wildebeest
24 "... neither fish ___ fowl!"
26 Tales of the gods
27 TV's Tarzan portrayer Ron
29 Where to get rubbed the right way?
34 Initial assault
35 Nipper's brand
37 Witness
39 Travels without a plan
40 Words of comprehension

41 Civil War soldier, for short
42 Earache
43 Leave in a hurry
46 Dismiss from consideration
47 Quit fasting
48 Degree held by many univ. professors
51 Snoopy's breed
53 Teller of falsehoods

55 Some defenders, in bridge columns
56 "___ which will live in infamy" (FDR)
57 Tips at sea
61 Future attorney's exam, briefly
62 "Do Ya" rock band
64 Krivoi ___, Ukraine
65 Beverage with scones
66 ___ Lanka

ACROSS

1 Literary shrugger
6 Veggie with eyes
10 "Egad!"
14 Nigerian currency
15 Opened one's eyes
16 Hoped-for review
17 Permission granted by a bishop
18 "Ah, me!"
19 Where Eve erred
20 Triumph, but just barely
22 Put on ___ (have an attitude)
23 ___ Lanka
24 Taker of a religious vow
26 Mighty hardwood
29 Depict unfairly, as statistics
32 Tit for ___
33 Short cut, perhaps
35 Turnpike turn-off
37 Pine exudation
41 Have a high-wire disaster
44 Beginning stage
45 Lightly burn
46 Uncontrollable masses
47 Grand Canyon viewing area
49 Actress Barrymore
51 Prime meridian letters
52 Registers, as a sale
56 You won't hear them from toadies
58 Dead fish carry one
59 Momentarily forget
65 Turning to the left

66 Atomic reactor
67 Diner staple
68 Isaac's eldest son
69 Subject of adoration
70 Feudal lord
71 Aerobics type
72 ___ out a living (just got by)
73 Support, as a college

DOWN

1 In a fresh way
2 Ride-seeker's cry
3 Legal claim on property
4 Jordanian majority
5 Lecherous goat-men
6 Kind of song
7 Game you can't play left-handed
8 Authoritative proclamation
9 Leave without leave
10 Heavy U.S. Olympics favorite
11 Ulnas' neighbors
12 Turn away, as one's eyes
13 Grammar subject
21 Clay of "American Idol" fame
25 Banjo picker Scruggs
26 Capital called Christiania until 1925
27 Unknown author, for short
28 Stolen item that's often returned
30 Halves of splits?
31 Smartened (up)
34 Common associates
36 Alpine conveyance
38 28-Down, in British slang

14

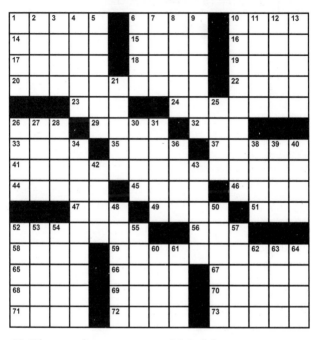

39 Mil. weapon that can cross an ocean
40 Digs made of twigs
42 Mayberry cell dweller
43 Venue for some basketball games
48 Child's make-believe dessert
50 Teeter
52 Screen parts
53 That is, in Latin
54 Exploding stars
55 Poke with a pin
57 Killed, as a dragon
60 Lotion substance
61 ___ one's way (proceed along)
62 More than passed
63 Like a scrubbed space mission
64 Had inside information

15

ACROSS

1 Hoods for monks
6 Blunders
11 Apparent moon path
14 Hang around for
15 Get by force
16 "A Christmas Carol" cry
17 Plead for compassionate treatment
19 Bio class letters
20 Prepares for a fight
21 Doesn't keep up
22 Niacin, for one
25 Footnote citation
27 Kasbah resident
28 Rescue ring
31 Bill holders
33 Samara-bearing trees
34 Try to get in
40 Academic challenge
41 A&E series involving tattoos
43 Brainy individual
48 Airline passenger's table
49 Drug that dulls the brain
50 Optimistic and then some
52 The Planet's strongest man
53 Veteran sailor
55 Team's top starting pitcher
56 What drought victims and farmers might do
61 Light stroke
62 Acclaim
63 Aerie tenant
64 Like many Canadian roads in winter
65 "Crazy" singer Cline
66 Allay by satisfying

DOWN

1 Airport lurker
2 Have a loan from
3 Tail or tongue movement
4 Able to be hoisted
5 High-wind producer
6 The Twins of the zodiac
7 "Olly, olly, ___ free"
8 Bireme blades
9 Govt. broadcasting watchdog
10 Future ham's home
11 Chafe
12 Texas law enforcer
13 Abyss
18 Fence around a racetrack
21 Tyler or Ullmann
22 Acid container
23 Eye part or flower
24 "The Handmaid's ___" (Margaret Atwood novel)
25 Systems of principles
26 Low men at the opera
29 ___ fatale
30 Wallach of "Cinderella Liberty"
32 Clay pigeons sport
35 One of two on a car
36 ___ segno (musical direction)
37 Absolutely necessary
38 Bourbon Street vegetable
39 Without ice
42 Use Grecian Formula
43 Syrup in the medicine cabinet

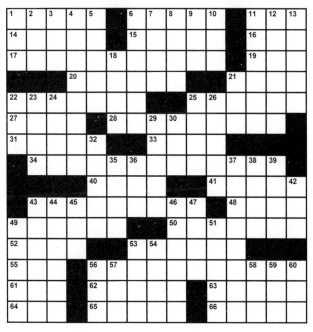

44 Number of feet between bases,
   in baseball
45 Machine gun syllable
46 Cunning
47 Kind of list with tasks
49 Animal with zebra-striped legs
51 Healing sites?
53 Potato chip seasoning
54 Nestling hawk
56 Get-up-and-go

57 TV brand name
58 Palindromic honorific
59 Breed
60 Word between surnames

ACROSS

1 Type of column or cord
7 Answer perfectly
10 Vegetative state
14 Bearlike
15 Nineties descriptor
16 Qaboos bin Said's country
17 Become enamored
19 Gown designer Wang
20 Old-school word meaning "For shame!"
21 Attack from all directions
22 Started the fire again
23 Superlative suffix
24 Dash sizes
25 Wrath
27 Cooperation roadblock
28 Kind of period or home
30 First light
32 Male meower
33 Picture within a picture
36 In an organized way
38 Step before setting the date
41 Bird in a clock
42 Certain Jamaican believer, for short
43 Aaron's 755 (Abbr.)
44 Certificate of indebtedness
46 Not phony
50 Fabled grasshopper rebuker
51 ___ out (barely get by)
52 Stop being apathetic
55 Chest-thumping critter
56 Former Russian despots

58 "The Most Happy ___" (Loesser musical)
60 Composition of some cups
61 Percussionist Puente
62 Become one with another
64 Check for errata
65 Creature in "The Lord of the Rings"
66 Income from ownership of wealth
67 Walesa of Polish politics
68 Butt remains
69 Doo-wop group member

DOWN

1 Do more than abide
2 Commend
3 Small land masses
4 Zero to Nero
5 Licorice-flavored seed
6 Russian revolutionary
7 On the edge of one's seat
8 Miner's peril
9 Object of a biblical trade
10 Harbor inlet
11 Folded brunch dish (Var.)
12 Orange flower
13 Gray area?
18 Temporary occupant
22 Echo
26 Steps on a ladder
29 Lyme disease transmitter
31 Holding areas for babies-to-be
34 Hangmen's ropes

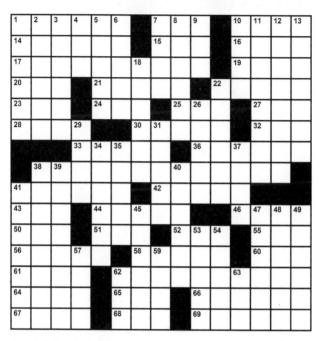

35 Garb for a kindergarten painting project

37 Thickener used in ice cream

38 Civil War general with famous facial hair

39 In seventh heaven

40 Fire bomb substance

41 Movable article of personal property

45 Alludes (to)

47 Gourmet's pleasure

48 For each one

49 Bank or library, at times

53 Name associated with the North Pole

54 Foot bones

57 IRA type

59 Design with acid

62 ___ few rounds (spar)

63 Bled in the laundry

ACROSS

1 What to do at the Wailing Wall
5 John of "Good Times"
9 "Last of the Red Hot ___" (Sophie Tucker)
14 Get under one's skin
15 Take one's turn in chess
16 Cockamamie
17 Passing announcement
18 Ovine utterance
19 Sort of, sort of
20 Port in the southern U.S.
23 Air pressure meas.
24 Be incorrect
25 Slow musical passage
28 Electrical pioneer Nikola
30 "There's more ..."
32 Biblical verb ending
33 Takes for granted
36 Approximating words
37 Traffic jam causes, sometimes
39 Mothers in woolly coats
41 Rating for a cheap hotel, perhaps
42 Long-jawed fish
43 Bygone orchard spray
44 Door fastener
48 Old name for the flu
50 Do some schussing
52 "Oh, I see"
53 Winter coating
57 Fabric fold
59 Twelfth Jewish month
60 Some stars have inflated ones
61 "The Good ___" (Buck book)
62 Site of exile for Napoleon
63 Ultimatum's end: "or ___"
64 Like a car without a muffler
65 Scottish girl
66 Source of pressure, perhaps

DOWN

1 On time
2 RNA sugar
3 Suspects' defenses
4 Hairy mountain sighting
5 Waves of grain color
6 Grinding tooth
7 Somewhat round
8 Words before "good example"
9 Gilbert and Sullivan operetta (with "The")
10 Jung's feminine component
11 Business operators
12 Pair's connector
13 Hemingway novel setting
21 Path of ___ resistance
22 Type of hound
26 "___ My Party"
27 "Well, well, well!"
29 Country abutting Vietnam
30 Muslim prince (Var.)
31 Shutterbug's attachment
34 Like some kisses and bases
35 Bone parallel to the radius
36 Creole cooking pod
37 Disease caused by vitamin B deficiency
38 Pac. state

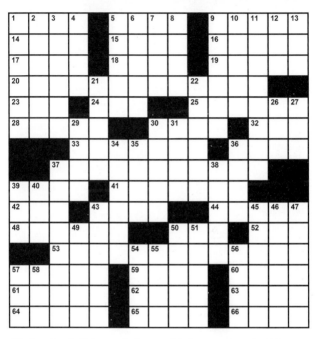

39 Party in a "which came first" debate
40 It can cause a draft
43 Passion's opposite
45 What a comb undoes
46 Make up your mind
47 Mooring rope
49 Land maps
50 Ticket taker's givebacks
51 Trees bearing valuable nuts

54 On an even ___ (stable)
55 "First Lady of Song" Fitzgerald
56 Escape through a crevice
57 Con's confines
58 Dweller on the Mekong River

ACROSS

1 Moose, in Europe
4 It's not the silence of the lambs
7 Barely defeat
10 Telly option
13 The N of NCO
14 Insurance company employee
16 "How ___ things?"
17 Superhero with a valet
19 ___ de plume
20 Oboe part
21 Caboose's place
22 Kind of clippers
24 Permit
26 Keeper
29 Professional charge
30 Member of the flock
32 Trigonometric function
33 In better order
35 Repair
36 They may be checked at the door
37 Web-based superhero?
40 Balaam's beast
42 Cure rawhide
43 Breakfast container
47 Finger pointer
49 Literary collection
50 Bath suds?
51 Detroit newspaper
53 Familiar episode
55 Fiction classification
56 Make a choice
58 Lavish celebration

59 Monopoly token choice
60 Superhero who liked Candy
64 "Antiques Roadshow" estimate
65 Rigby of song
66 List ender, briefly
67 "Waking ___ Devine" (1998 film)
68 The EPA banned it in 1972
69 Place with fortified swine?
70 Actor Tommy ___ Jones

DOWN

1 Attach a bud to a new plant
2 Her songs lure Rhine boatmen
3 Genuflected
4 Prohibit officially
5 Muscle misery
6 This minute
7 Tandoori-baked bread
8 Wrathful emotion
9 Type of boa
10 Kicked (about)
11 Work shoes
12 Driveway material
15 Language kin of Hindi
18 Old Tokyo
23 Decorative border
25 Shed a few tears
27 Use a spoon
28 Publicans of old Rome
31 Columnist, e.g.
34 Distributor
35 Low-lying wetland
38 Take a chance
39 Food-thickening agent

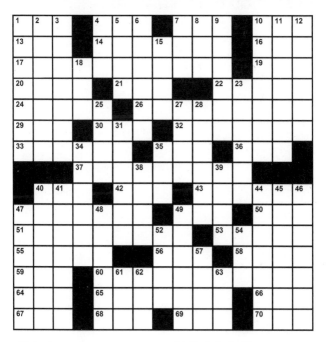

40 Land amount
41 Like many candles
44 Apple coating, come Halloween
45 Cry like a mourner
46 What a sinner may do
47 Crocheted blanket
48 Shot out, as lava
49 Quakers in the forest
52 Pop in the mouth?

54 Easily bruised item
57 Jog
61 Word with "Faithful" or "Glory"
62 Volleyball obstacle
63 Amusingly ironic, as humor

ACROSS

1 Wanders around
5 Cosa Nostra leaders
10 Completely infatuated
14 Oil cartel's letters
15 Crawled out of bed
16 The backup one is B
17 Box, but not seriously
18 Kidney-related
19 Cajun cooking pod
20 Yegg
23 The largest share possible
24 Not as healthy
25 When sold separately
26 ___-tzu
27 Paper towel layer
28 Often-candied vegetable
31 Puffing, as on a cigarette
33 Ranch or farm
36 Harrison role, familiarly
37 Spoiler of the whole bunch
40 Midvoyage
42 Magnate
43 Coffin contents
46 Broiled sushi fish
47 Respected degree
50 Mt. Rushmore moniker
51 Sax type
54 Sans friendliness
56 Last of an annual dozen, briefly
57 Difficult one to deal with
60 February 14 deity
62 Mumbai's land

63 Funnyman Carvey
64 Word with "mortals" or "formality"
65 Passes through slowly
66 Result of pulling the plug?
67 Norse tales
68 Dada painter Max
69 Prescription quantity

DOWN

1 Scuttlebutt
2 Fill with outrage
3 With an unwillingness to pay heed
4 Rocky slope accumulation
5 Singer Vikki
6 Square measure
7 Explorer ___ de Leon
8 Japanese seaport
9 Pick out
10 Central mail bureau
11 Ten-time AL Gold Glove winner for the Tigers
12 "The Wizard of Oz" star
13 Where "is to" is used
21 Place for 43-Across
22 P, to the Greeks
29 ___ Deco
30 Track and field event
32 Potter's furnace
33 Curser's mouthwash?
34 ___ minute (soon)
35 Stout freshwater fish
37 Tape again
38 "The Raven" penner

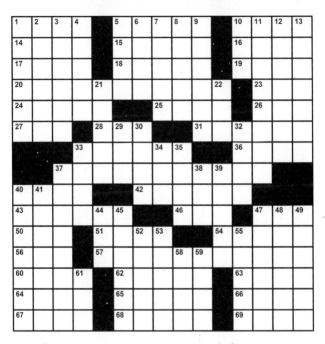

39 Salk vaccine target
40 The scholarly world
41 Recovered from a bender (with "up")
44 Pulled up a chair
45 Plaza's pigtailed pixie
47 Yum-Yum's operetta (with "The")
48 They're often pulled at night
49 Shipboard affirmative

52 One who fixes a piano
53 City of northern Utah
55 Like secret messages
58 Hula dancers sway them
59 Throw, as dice
61 "Finding Nemo" setting

13 FIRST-AID KIT · By Kathy Whitlock

ACROSS

1 Backbone of a ship
5 "The Terminator" character Connor
10 Development unit, perhaps
14 Concerning, on a memo
15 Seek redemption
16 Address for a queen
17 Place to doodle
19 Osiris's wife
20 "___ guy walks into a bar ..."
21 "You, there, on the boat!"
22 Light green plums
24 Suffix for "east"
25 This may be the end to alcohol?
26 Kind of workout
28 Fix, as a driveway
30 Five after three?
32 "Double Fantasy" Grammy winner
33 Hospitable wreath
35 ___ Paulo
36 Unremarkable
37 Product-holding plastic
40 Braving the waves
42 Creator of Atticus Finch
43 Relaxing site
44 Limbo need
45 Gold unit
47 Indonesian boats
51 Denounce
53 Card "in the hole"
55 One-eighty from NNE
56 Siberian forest
57 Atmosphere
58 ___ Beta Kappa
59 Israeli circle dance
60 Abundant harvest
63 Cato's 2550
64 Astrological ram
65 Paris pop
66 Disorderly heap
67 Performed, in Shakespeare
68 Certain assents

DOWN

1 Puss
2 Audience demand
3 Off-base
4 Low place?
5 Investment firm Goldman ___
6 Awaiting visitors
7 Cordlike
8 Assemblage of miscellaneous info
9 Flies very close to the ground
10 "Adios, ___"
11 It has precedents
12 California fruits
13 Minimum borders?
18 Capital of Taiwan
23 Getty Museum purchase
26 Thickening agent used in ice cream
27 Pigeon sound
29 Spanish stew
31 "___ bad moon rising" (1969 song lyric)
34 Capital of Pakistan

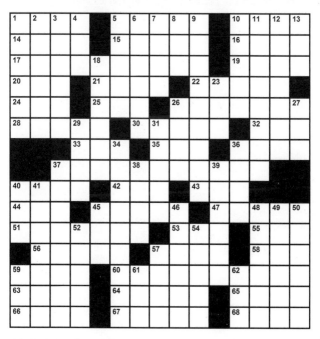

36 Reminder of a wound
37 Alpine dogs ("with Saint")
38 Slender-billed sea bird
39 Come within sight
40 Disney acquisition
41 Principe's island partner
45 Resource to be tapped?
46 Brownish grays
48 Fish-eating hawk

49 How some things may get washed
50 Pilfers
52 Radio tuners
54 Comber's comb
57 In the center of
59 "That's curious ..."
61 Spoon-bending mentalist Geller
62 One who gets plaudits for averting audits

27

FICKLE TICKLE · By Cameron Rooney

ACROSS

1 Wild and crazy
5 Ottoman Empire title
10 Does a hit man's job
14 Diva's performance, sometimes
15 "___ a Grecian Urn"
16 Lot measurement
17 Sole food?
20 Flowery verse
21 Deadly insect
22 Synopsis starter and ender?
23 Decline
26 Syllable sung before "la la"
27 Bit of skin art, slangily
30 Becomes compost
32 Where Guernseys graze
34 Light at the disco
36 Ready to travel
39 Davenport dweller
40 Type of financial theory
42 North Carolina fort
44 Silver medalist's place
45 Ease up
47 Neither's companion
48 Whiffenpoof's school
52 "Bon" or "mon" follower
53 Sounds at doctors' checkups
55 Swedish rug
57 Anti-prohibition
58 Descendant of Noah's eldest
61 Rein for Rover
63 Defunct flag symbol
67 The number one guy?
68 Single-masted vessel
69 Will beneficiary
70 Frosted Flakes mascot
71 Cantankerous
72 Scores for free throws

DOWN

1 Stun gun, e.g.
2 Melodic
3 Most genteel
4 Runs off at the mouth
5 "The Conqueror Worm" poet
6 Do simple arithmetic
7 Mo. of many Virgos
8 Apparatus for lifting
9 Makes irate
10 Clumsy lummoxes
11 Capital of Sierra Leone
12 Bank add-on
13 Put one's cheeks down?
18 Caustic cleaner
19 Paddington or Grand Central
24 Group that votes alike
25 Pecking parts
28 Lawyers' gp.
29 Half a score
31 Private leader?
33 Harold of songdom
35 Boisterous
37 Major Hollywood attraction
38 Interior designer's doing
40 Amulet
41 Small craft
42 Thing with cups and hooks
43 Sleep state initials

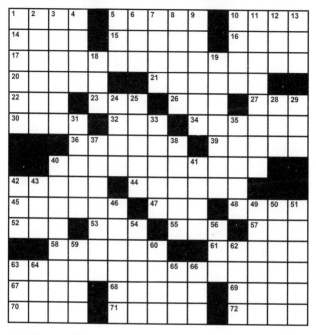

46 What you slake
49 Become conscious
50 Nielsen or Uggams
51 Heavenly airs
54 Musty
56 "The Greatest" via self-proclamation
59 TV award
60 He lived 905 years
62 It may bounce off walls

63 It goes right over your head
64 Fuss and feathers
65 Morse code E
66 Cloak-and-dagger figure

ACROSS

1 Blow from a cat-o'-nine-tails
5 Stinging remarks
10 Rough guess
14 The 29th state
15 Protruding window
16 Be laid up with
17 Oxymoronic physical description
19 Sword not intended to harm
20 2006 FIFA World Cup winners
21 Where life is a grind?
22 Notch made by a saw
23 Library stamps
25 Dual-purpose couch
27 One-person performances
29 ___ Island (immigrants' site)
32 Identifies correctly
35 Allow
39 More than displeasure
40 Tokyo's name, once
41 Umbrella-toting "Batman" villain
42 Part of a wedding ceremony
43 Narcissist's problem
44 "... nothing to fear but fear ___"
45 Clothing store department
46 Peter, in Spain
48 Software test version
50 Artillery unit member
54 Foot-longs in school?
58 They make waves
60 It may be found in a ring
62 On again, as a lantern

63 Glassmaker's mixture
64 Oxymoronic place to work
66 Experience the effects of
67 More standoffish
68 "Beauty ___ the eye ..."
69 Sound partner?
70 "___ once was a man from ..."
71 Is unable to

DOWN

1 Fatty acid, e.g.
2 Heart line
3 Perspire
4 Bareheaded
5 He lived with Tarzan
6 Jack-in-the-pulpit, for one
7 Unyielding
8 Lovely, as a signorina
9 With an ulterior motive
10 Tel Aviv coin
11 Broadcaster's oxymoron
12 Declare to be true
13 Cattleman's product
18 Tenderfoot
24 February forecast, sometimes
26 "___ here long?"
28 Cozy places to stay
30 Collar straightener
31 Closes a rip
32 Mild protest
33 Periphery
34 Oxymoron from Charlie Brown
36 Sweet sixteen, e.g.
37 It's often screwed up

38 One who'll always be in
41 Subatomic bit
45 Evil
47 Steal livestock
49 Filet mignon, when served with lobster
51 Like seven games Nolan Ryan pitched
52 Important historical period
53 Cordage fiber

55 Woman in a "Paint Your Wagon" song
56 Castor bean product
57 Surgeon's insertion
58 Snuffs out
59 High-pressure ___
61 Look lustfully
65 Raw smelting material

ACROSS

1 English bloke
5 Oahu greeting
10 ___ en scene (stage setting)
14 Put to an oilstone
15 Drink like dogs
16 Mischievous kids
17 Untoppable rating
18 Prolonged campaign
19 TV ad
20 Certain diner employee
23 Permission
24 Nipper appeared in its ad
25 Eight ball start
27 "Heir" attachment
28 Close by, to poets
32 Bearish
34 Like some threats
36 Inventory listing
37 Some missiles
40 Vampire's tooth
42 Poor imitator
43 Animated film with Manny the mammoth
46 Thumb-to-pinkie measure
47 Lengthen unnecessarily
50 Tabby's suitor
51 Recognizes in a lineup
53 Overplay a scene
55 Aged
60 Auld lang ___
61 Beachgoer's need
62 Muse of history
63 Redding of soul
64 Projecting window
65 Munster mister
66 The Amish, for one
67 Rips to pieces
68 Middle Eastern gulf

DOWN

1 Gliding step in ballet
2 Foofaraws
3 Vexes
4 Dukes and earls
5 "And another thing ..."
6 Dragon's domicile
7 Page with commentary
8 More humongous
9 Short synopsis
10 Paste used in Japanese soups
11 Rude
12 City or river in Washington
13 Suffix that maximizes
21 In shape
22 Pullman, for one
26 Fine stone
29 Sequel-to-a-sequel designation
30 Model airplane kit requirement
31 Cannabis plants
33 Third base coach's hand movement
34 "Luka" singer Suzanne
35 Sound of a defective faucet
37 Memory trigger
38 Word before Khan
39 Octet plus one
40 ___ to be tied
41 Altar boy

44 Booking for musicians
45 Newspaper VIP
47 Combined, as assets
48 Apparel
49 Remove antlers
52 Make sound asleep?
54 Brown shade
56 Twiggy digs
57 One of the Gemini

58 Take advice
59 Pipes with bends
60 Emergency call to the Coast Guard

17 | ALL GOOD THINGS MUST COME TO AN . . . .
By Gary Cooper

ACROSS

1 ABC rival
4 Piece of accurate information
8 Cat's quarry
13 Guggenheim stuff
14 Cupid's missile
15 Force forward
16 Poker verb
17 Prefix meaning "straight"
18 Hemp source
19 Die
22 Contribute to the mix
23 "___ many cooks spoil the broth"
24 Directly, in directions
27 Fleeces
31 Practice that won't leave you in stitches?
33 Big Band or Prohibition
34 Behave like Gloomy Gus
36 Con men pull them
37 Be in need of repair
41 Readily available
43 "And then there were ___"
44 Syllable from the stands
47 Weaken with water
49 Eighteen, usually
52 Culbertson of bridge fame
53 Type
55 Sausage alternative
56 Finishes
60 Brother of Moses
63 Becomes less dense
64 Tree marketed in December
65 Fauna's companion
66 Sure success
67 AK-47 relative
68 Kind of basin or wave
69 Love's antithesis
70 Superman's foe Luthor

DOWN

1 Rush down in big quantities
2 Owner of a stud farm
3 Unwaveringly
4 Agonize (over)
5 With the bow, to a violinist
6 Shelter for doves
7 Between, quaintly
8 Jefferson City's state
9 Forget to include
10 Co. with brown uniforms
11 It'll float your boat
12 Letter with a right angle
14 Pro basketball game site
20 Title for Churchill
21 Suffix with "invent"
24 Shameful and shocking
25 Wear and tear
26 Printer measures
28 Ref's cousin
29 Crossword clue direction
30 Fishing reel winder
32 Insist on payment from
35 White-tailed sea eagle
38 Greek letter T
39 Unrequired
40 Frat party dispenser

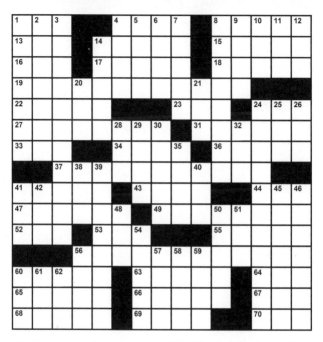

41 Verse on a vase?
42 Diddly-squat
45 Struggle painfully (over)
46 Jimi with an afro
48 State tree of Massachusetts
50 Embarrass
51 PC linking system
54 Two-masted sailing vessel
56 Mrs. Dithers of "Blondie"

57 LaBeouf of "Transformers"
58 Limo window feature
59 "Measure twice, cut ___"
60 Opposite of fore
61 "Arabian Nights" figure, ___ Baba
62 Attachment for 30-Down

DRILL, BABY, DRILL · By Kathy Whitlock

ACROSS

1 Favoritism or discrimination
5 Mantra
10 Monopoly need
14 Rainfall measurement unit
15 Rapscallion
16 Young troublemakers
17 Charlie Brown tormentor
18 Good smell from the kitchen
19 Quibbling quarrel
20 Honeymooner with 39-Across?
23 Acting in a play, right now
24 Fountain treats
27 Witnesses
28 Experimental flyer
32 ___ shot (drummer's quickie)
34 Jamaican music genre
35 Wolfe of whodunits
36 Breast-beating creature
39 Canine examiner
42 Dawn dampness
43 On its way
45 "7 Faces of Dr. ___"
46 ___ Lanka
48 Original model
51 Drying kiln
54 Oyster's prize
55 Gives personal assurance
58 When you're told to open wide?
62 ___ John's (Domino's competitor)
64 Distributed cards
65 Heal completely
66 Help with a heist
67 Without worldly wisdom
68 Wearing apparel
69 ___-in-waiting (princess's attendant)
70 "Over the Rainbow" co-composer Harold
71 Puts two and two together

DOWN

1 "The Hobbit" hero Baggins
2 Preserves, as remains
3 Level charges at
4 Shady lawyer
5 Diet guru Jenny
6 Yellow jacket's cousin
7 In a state of excitement
8 Shot up with Novocain
9 Sign of grief
10 Contempt
11 Drove forward
12 Number cruncher, for short
13 Ballpark figure (Abbr.)
21 Member of a certain Jewish sect
22 Little mischief-maker
25 Sped down the street
26 Load cargo
29 Block legally
30 Enjoy snow-covered slopes
31 Soviet news service: ITAR-___
33 Run in the heat?
36 When the boss wants it
37 French dad
38 Pitched one's tent and settled in

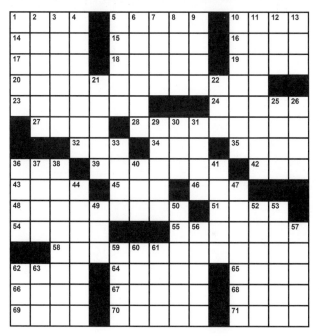

40 Vote of dissent
41 Rainbow fish
44 Husky, as a voice
47 Former Chrysler head Lee
49 Common tree
50 Develop by gradual changes
52 Ought to
53 Four of a kind
56 Time and again

57 Tool-storage buildings
59 Bart's teacher Krabappel
60 Get closer to
61 Rear of a plane
62 Buddy
63 Lawyers' org.

ACROSS

1 Senegal's capital
6 Greek P
9 Ride a bike
14 Useful
15 Clumsy clod
16 Walker of whiskey
17 Kewpie and Barbie
18 ___ for tat
19 Totally absurd
20 Two images on one television
23 Peas keeper?
24 Take in nourishment
25 Like some tires
27 Oil-measuring rod
32 More than want
33 "How was ___ know?"
34 Barkin or DeGeneres
36 Throat-soothing candies
39 Didn't part with
41 Grows weary
43 GI's off-base offense
44 One making introductory remarks
46 Likely to err
48 "All Things Considered" broadcaster
49 Loosen, as laces
51 Frets, in modern parlance
53 Army person
56 Dr. Seuss's "Sam ___"
57 Demolitionist's charge
58 Begin major construction
64 "The ___ Suspects"

66 Wordplay groaner
67 ___ far (exceed the limits)
68 Capital of Switzerland (Var.)
69 Gorged oneself
70 "… with ___ of thousands!"
71 Undoes, as an edit
72 "That smarts!"
73 Theater or library admonishment

DOWN

1 Bombs that don't explode
2 At the acme of
3 "Thou shalt not ___"
4 Nations united
5 Say again
6 Campus mil. group
7 It could receive permanent damage?
8 Seldom's opposite
9 Did pull-ups
10 Partner of yang
11 Some police operations
12 Hawaiian party site
13 Make corrections to
21 Long-legged wader
22 Centuries and centuries
26 Doris Day song title word after "Que"
27 Site of Hans Brinker's heroism
28 Checklist unit
29 TV, movies, comics, etc.
30 152, in Roman numerals
31 Joanna of "Growing Pains"
35 Hair-removal brand name

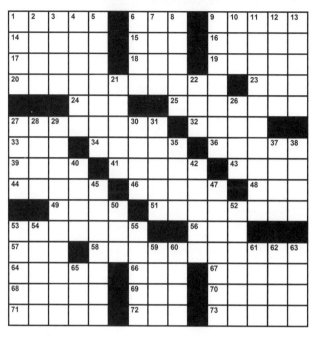

37 John Paul II's title
38 Some 35mm cameras
40 Work behind the bar
42 Parsley unit
45 Stuff you can munch on
47 Riot squad's supply
50 Opposite of 'neath
52 Kiss
53 Theater-floor litter

54 Beginning phase
55 Best way to maintain one's credit rating
59 Cougar or Jaguar
60 Had a gut feeling
61 The 45th of 50
62 Raid the refrigerator
63 "The lady ___ protest too much"
65 "Soldier" insect

ACROSS

1 Ends partner
5 Former embryo
10 Ruin
13 "It's ___ a pleasure"
14 As mad as a wet hen
15 ___ fide (authentic)
16 Soldiers on foot, collectively
18 Charged-up atoms
19 Vein extraction
20 Dilapidated dwelling
22 In an unacceptable way
26 DiFranco of music
27 Rectangular groove
28 "... ___ he drove out of sight ..."
29 She's "sweet as apple cider," in song
30 Bed frame strips
32 Rainbow-shaped
36 Soup can flaw
38 Many crossword puzzles have one
40 Its roe is a delicacy
41 Uncredited actor
43 Follows commands
45 Historical period
46 Space bar neighbor, on some keyboards
48 Writer Waugh
49 1960s TV Tarzan Ron
50 Pool wear
55 With "Beach," a Florida city
56 Tactical tennis shot
57 Scott Turow book about Harvard Law School
58 Like some medicine bottles
64 Moss on the runway
65 Major hub of Japan
66 Actress Hathaway
67 U.S. Airways info
68 Like a lover's nothings
69 Connery or Lennon

DOWN

1 ___-Wan Kenobi
2 Animal house
3 Type of chemical sprayed on plants
4 Traffic jam
5 ___ as a fiddle
6 Make a mistake
7 Mai ___ (cocktail)
8 Wombs
9 Elmo's street
10 Demi or Roger
11 One-year record
12 Like some smokers' voices
15 Sharp-tasting ales
17 More than wants
21 Scarlett's home
22 S&P 500, for one
23 John of "Atlas Shrugged"
24 Boise state
25 Pledge drive freebie
26 White House intern, e.g.
31 Refine metal
33 Supermodel's asset, often
34 Countesses' counterparts

35 June 1944 event
37 Walk all over
39 Ogling one
42 ___ mater
44 Carve or model
47 Colors slightly
50 Said something
51 Was victorious in
52 "___ man with seven wives"

53 "When pigs fly!"
54 Jones and Ephron
59 '50s campaign button name
60 Drain cleaner ingredient
61 Part of e-mail addresses
62 "Little Miss Muffet sat ___ ..."
63 Marshy land

BASIC COUNT · By Dennis Mooney

ACROSS

1 "Please" to a Hamburger
6 Lane who was married to Xavier Cugat
10 Court action
14 Lend ___ (listen)
15 Group of two
16 Backside
17 1982 Francis Ford Coppola film
20 Sheet of matted cotton
21 "Miss Saigon" setting
22 Broke bread
23 Reply to "Should we?"
24 Mail a payment
28 Popular carpet type
30 Design style popular in the '20s and '30s
32 Elizabethan favorite Sir Walter
35 Use needle and thread
36 Film with Audrey Hepburn and Albert Finney
40 Color quality
41 Turning muscle
42 Groups of nine
45 Breakfast chef's creation
49 Iron or copper, e.g.
50 Beginning for "normal" or "legal"
52 "It's ___-win situation!"
53 Sills, Price, and others
56 No ifs, ___, or buts
57 Ringling Brothers offering
61 Thieves' booty
62 Mid-month, to Caesar
63 Tractor man John
64 Farm females
65 Tuna-and-cheese sandwich
66 Appeases hunger

DOWN

1 Tree with a gourdlike fruit
2 From nature, not nurture
3 Be unsteady
4 Heaviest U.S. President
5 Commit a faux pas
6 Let through the turnstile
7 Computer-storage units
8 Currency of Thailand
9 First family's residence
10 Aspiring doc's program
11 Pasture
12 Musical aptitude, of a sort
13 Museum display
18 Feudal system big shot
19 Male red deer
23 Turn over a new ___
25 City in Arizona
26 Chilled, in a way
27 Pull to the garage
29 Sib for a sis
30 Turkish title of respect (Var.)
31 Pretentious speech
33 Winged Greek god with a bow
34 "The Addams Family" cousin
36 Adjust the piano
37 Departed
38 "Arrivederci ___"

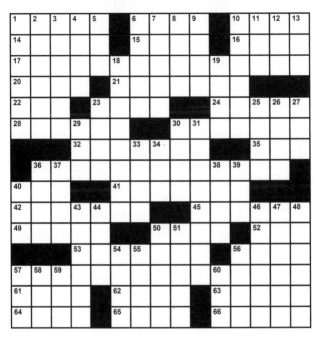

39 Mine find
40 Dress bottom
43 Studio supports
44 Skin-soothing ingredient
46 Surgical knife
47 Stand the test of time
48 Coin flips
50 Comic strip segment
51 Feeling of anxiety

54 Proper's partner
55 Busch Gardens attraction
56 Geometric product
57 Everyday article
58 "Hee ___"
59 Regret
60 Selects from a photo lineup

ACROSS

1 Bighorn bleats
5 Sunblock lotion ingredient
9 Duel units
14 Pitcher-turned-slugger Babe
15 Hayloft's location
16 Put to shame
17 Square footage measure
18 Debtor's burden
19 Given to back talk
20 Ice cream flavor
23 "___ Little Indians" (1965 thriller)
24 Positioned accurately
25 Use the mind's eye
27 Made use of a sofa
28 Play the market
32 "Dungeons & Dragons" creatures
33 Gentleman caller, e.g.
34 Woodwind section members
35 Ice cream flavor
38 Surgery reminders
40 Propelled, in a way
41 Old sailors
42 Trustbuster's concern
44 Rogue
47 Gymnast's getup
49 Nit layer
51 Cooking utensil
52 Ice cream flavor
56 "Time is ___ Side" (New Kids on the Block)
58 "And lead us not ___ ..."
59 At the pinnacle

60 Shampoo follow-up
61 Walking aid
62 Perfect for picking
63 Audition segment
64 "___ the night before ..."
65 Many a Jonas Brothers fan

DOWN

1 Modified leaves on flower stems
2 ___ borealis (northern lights)
3 Enjoyed the diner
4 Dairy Queen treat
5 Fit for the task
6 Put down, as carpet
7 Cookie with a floral design on it
8 Feelings of boredom
9 Former Ottoman title
10 League of legal eagles (Abbr.)
11 Like some stomachs or stoves
12 Perfumer's extract
13 Shrinking violet's problem
21 Numbskulls
22 Prime meridian std.
26 Spoil, as milk
29 "She loves me ___"
30 Churchill symbol
31 Trial's companion
33 Stuttgart sausage
34 Spots on peacock feathers
35 Voice between bass and tenor
36 Sajak or Boone
37 "Able was I ___ I saw Elba"
38 Drunken states

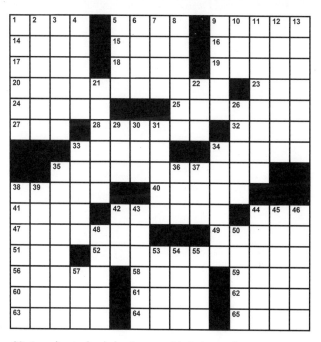

39 According to church doctrine
42 Group of vineyards
43 One who's hooked
44 Eliminating game in a trophy competition
45 Tilted
46 Excavate further
48 "It's ___ country"
50 Dizzying abstract genre
53 What rodents do

54 Sicilian peak
55 Agile deer
57 Seabee's mil. branch

ACROSS

1 Persona non ___
6 Winter resort rentals
10 Cause friction
13 More maneuverable at sea
14 The Emerald Isle
15 Math term
16 Commodity rating
18 "Black Beauty" writer Sewell
19 ___ boom bah
20 It turns litmus paper red
21 Baseball infielder, at times
23 Kitchen item
25 Reduced in intensity
26 Avian mimic
27 "I Hope You Dance" singer Womack
30 Versified salute
31 Slovenly abode
33 It gets the pot going
34 "The Simpsons" character Flanders
35 A considerable distance
37 Boxer's initials?
38 Sax player's purchase
40 Lennon's widow Yoko
41 About 4,047 square meters
43 Something that's illegal to drop
44 Golfer's goal
45 One religion in Haiti
47 "Where Eagles ___"
51 Summer refresher
53 Dick, Batman's Robin
55 Cricket umpire's call
56 Small singing bird
57 "___ duck walks in to a bar ..."
58 Get ___ the ground floor
59 Talent for agriculture
62 Bettor's numbers
63 New Testament book
64 Like the boondocks
65 Edinburgh refusal
66 Talk back
67 Sharp mountain ridge

DOWN

1 Plaster of Paris ingredient
2 Seldom-seen thing
3 Like a phoenix out of the ashes
4 Private eye, slangily
5 Fields of study
6 More than forgetful
7 Notorious pirate Captain ___
8 Cousin of rage
9 Seafarer's instrument
10 Downloadable cell phone alert
11 Not necessary
12 Like Lincoln and Santa Claus, notably
15 Epic chronicle
17 In a very unfriendly way
22 Doubleday and Yokum
24 Agcy. that shoots for the stars
28 Having roof overhangs
29 Furthermore
32 Pack up and go
35 Amazon predator
36 Portend

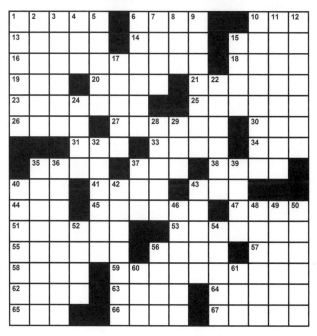

37 Sis sibling
39 Whirling waters
40 Point of view
42 Poisonous emission
43 Ponti's Sophia
46 Shrek's Fiona is one
48 Promise confidently
49 Be a boarder of
50 Render capable

52 Beachgoers get them
54 Cavities in bones
56 Adds moisture to
60 DVD player maker
61 "Ben-___" (1959 Best Picture)

ACROSS

1 Nero's wear
5 Acknowledged applause
10 A little wet
14 Nutmeg covering
15 Succumb to wind and water
16 Middle Eastern prince
17 Island in Indonesia
18 Big name in whiskey
19 "___ Enchanted Evening"
20 They're behind certain actions
23 Hyde Park pram pusher
24 Dealers' customers
25 Chore
28 Pool-table surface material
30 Potatoes accompaniment
31 Puts on a really happy face
33 Compete
36 What to expect for a much lower price
40 ___ down (disappoint)
41 World book?
42 Manhattan, e.g.
43 Highlands dialect
44 Caravan animals
46 Looking down on
49 Queen's headgear
51 Strategic military advantage
57 Musial of baseball
58 Lines of departure?
59 Throw off
60 Anguine fishes
61 Home made of hides
62 Rounds and the like

63 Not great or awful
64 ___ Rock (Uluru)
65 Shuttle's org.

DOWN

1 Chanel No. 5 alternative
2 Kind of hygiene
3 Decorated with gold
4 Make an enemy
5 Trailing
6 Hunter of the stars
7 Cause of wrinkles
8 Yellow cheese
9 Dealer's model
10 Partner of cease
11 "Don't make ___!" ("Freeze!")
12 Silent performer
13 Iron, as clothes
21 Appeared in the paper
22 Oklahoma city
25 "The Last Command" Oscar-winner Jannings
26 "Pandora's Box" painter Magritte
27 Whitewater transport
28 Helpful Web pages
29 Flightless bird from Down Under
31 Tree stump
32 Paleozoic ___
33 Workshop squeezer
34 "___ have to do"
35 They may be bloodshot
37 Tougher to find
38 "___ about time!"

39 Succotash component
43 "Still ..."
44 Political movements
45 Spot for a tattoo, perhaps
46 Braying equines
47 Broad-winged hawk
48 Some birthstones
49 Blather
50 Put in a mausoleum

52 Ninth letter of the Greek alphabet
53 Debated wedding-vow word
54 1815 Jane Austen novel
55 Basket's edges
56 Plato's portico

ACROSS

1 Dogie snagger
6 Voice in the choir
10 Dark red
14 Stomach lining problem
15 Bouncer's station
16 Overseas title (Var.)
17 Very tidy
19 Cut in a skirt
20 Subtract
21 Pant waist inserts
23 Guilty, e.g.
25 Heineken bottle symbol
26 Children's card game
29 Makes a miscalculation
31 Evoke, as a response
35 Summer drink suffix
36 Little lice
38 Union Civil War general George
39 Spotless
43 Form of address for a tot
44 Blunted dueling sword
45 Dusk, poetically
46 Worry persistently
48 Rodgers's collaborator
50 Street crossers, sometimes (Abbr.)
51 Be a star
53 Track habitue
55 Sewing machine parts
59 In the same place, in footnotes
63 Indian attire
64 Pristine
66 Rainfall-challenged
67 Subject of a sentence
68 Large-eyed tree climber
69 Glass designer Lalique
70 Dead set against
71 South African golfer Els

DOWN

1 Bergman's "Casablanca" role
2 Opposite the wind
3 Great quantity
4 Arrange, as a meeting
5 Divine communicator
6 Orthodontists' org.
7 Easy run
8 Breaks one's back
9 Highly decorative
10 Doughy desserts
11 Uncomely citrus fruit?
12 Elegantly stylish
13 Tries the truffles
18 Breastbones
22 Pheasant ragout
24 Face the day
26 Screwball
27 Improvise
28 Orchestra section
30 Type of bacterial infection
32 Feed at a fête for a fee
33 Ran in neutral
34 Soon-to-be adults
37 Gymnast's beads
40 Capital of South Australia
41 Barely beat, with "out"

50

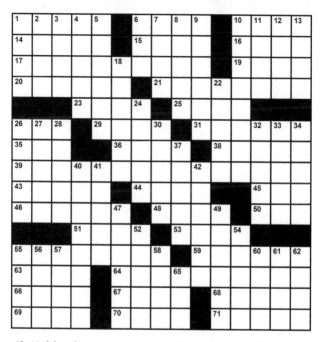

42 Medal-worthy
47 City of central Kansas
49 Capillary, e.g.
52 Screwtape, in "The Screwtape Letters"
54 Bathroom floor installer
55 Pre-Russian Revolution ruler
56 Facing extinction
57 The Auld Sod
58 Censor's target

60 Broadway's "___ Yankees"
61 Small needle case
62 A ___ formality
65 Folk rocker DiFranco

26 DIRECTOR'S CUT · By Armond Greene

ACROSS

1 Snappy comeback
7 Tiger sound
11 T.S. Eliot's favorite animal?
14 More convenient
15 Impulse
16 Fussy bustle
17 Pigment-deficient animal
18 Gulf War missile
19 Urban vermin
20 Prepares (for)
23 Concert, essentially
26 Tire gauge reading (Abbr.)
27 Checklist detail
28 Turpentine, e.g.
31 Far from colorful
34 Patronize a diner
35 Silk Road continent
37 Grammy winner Keys
41 Acts
44 Landlocked European land
45 Cut from the same cloth
46 Sports Illustrated's Sportsman of the Century
47 ___ Mawr, Pa.
49 Dreamed up
51 Eclectic assortment
54 Hither and ___
56 Parched
57 Prepare for romance, in a way
62 Cloning material
63 Essential nutrient
64 One who takes too much interest in his work?

68 Humpty Dumpty, e.g.
69 Part of a chain
70 To be specific
71 Wade opponent
72 Smaller amount
73 Tweeter output

DOWN

1 Cell stuff, briefly
2 Underwater electricity source
3 File flap
4 Prayer
5 Thinker Descartes
6 Gait faster than a walk
7 Oxidizes
8 Prom corsage, often
9 Flulike ailment
10 Cincinnati's nine
11 Stone size
12 "Still waters run deep," for example
13 Clan emblem
21 Pole to extend a sail
22 Shin bone
23 Cancels a dele
24 Midway alternative
25 Gas unit on the autobahn
29 Lowest point
30 Test format, sometimes
32 Gung-ho and then some
33 "Leave me ___!"
36 "Just as I thought!"
38 Forklift burden
39 Dynamo's antithesis

40 Indirect remark
42 Man with a mission?
43 ___ out a living (barely making do)
48 Hose
50 Take for granted
51 More unusual
52 Jargon of a particular field
53 Public persona
55 Porcine replies

58 Marathoner's burden
59 Buffalo's lake
60 Easter event
61 Winter Palace VIP
65 Yank's Civil War foe
66 Shape of many six-sided rooms
67 Bread with ham, often

ACROSS

1 Capital of Oman
7 "For pity's sake!"
11 Prefix with "solve" or "respect"
14 Like many rumors
15 "On the house"
17 Sunni counterpart
18 Like a scab
19 ___ Aviv, Israel
20 Freelance
22 Before, palindromically
23 One of a deadly septet
24 Drunkard
25 Become compost
26 ___ culpa
27 Second half of an audiotape
31 Builder's area
33 Thieves' work
34 Costing nothing
40 Some golf clubs
41 Spike and Pinky
43 Like some starfish arms
46 Maximal suffix
49 Billy the Kid slayer Garrett
50 Adam's mate
51 Accountant, briefly
52 Make a misstep
53 Parlor
59 "Gimme ___!" (start of an Iowa State cheer)
60 Crazily
61 Nation of Roma
63 Got off ___ (avoided punishment)
64 Regret deeply
65 Bedtime, for some
66 Works from Wordsworth
67 Tiny amount

DOWN

1 Summons, as strength
2 Cowardly
3 Heel type
4 Dernier ___ (the latest fashion)
5 Developmental disorder
6 "Itsy Bitsy ___ Weenie Yellow Polka Dot Bikini"
7 Aunt of Prince Harry
8 Roller coaster feature
9 Teenager's breakout
10 Deliberately avoid
11 Most parched
12 "May ___?" (request to leave)
13 ___ jail (imprisoned)
16 ___ so forth
21 Some forensic evidence
27 Visualize
28 "There is no ___ team"
29 "Spring forward, fall back" abbr.
30 And others, in brief
32 Kuwait potentate
33 "___ Pinafore"
35 Paid athlete
36 Depleted
37 Rustic hotel
38 Withdrew formally
39 Longing
42 Grooved, as a muscle

43 Fight temptation
44 Demonstrate clearly
45 Boards, as a plane
46 Prefix with "sphere" or "friendly"
47 Turns bad
48 Large gong
54 Tit for ___
55 Data, informally
56 Overly bookish sort

57 ___ club (singing group)
58 Some loaves
62 "___ my brother's keeper?"

ACROSS

1 St. Peter's station
5 "Last of the Red Hot ___" (Tucker)
10 Device that's sprung
14 Took unfair advantage of
15 Jong with a "Fear of Fifty"
16 Thank-you item
17 Do a batting-practice chore
18 Voile used to make curtains
19 End of a lion's tail
20 The sun peeking through the clouds, to some
23 What a cellist has to do before playing
24 Slowly wear away, as a cliff face
25 Joint between the thigh and shin
26 Hindu Mr.
27 Finished working, for good (Abbr.)
28 Thick Swedish rug
31 Break for students
33 Corrects text
36 Boy Scout recitation
37 Square dance song
40 ___ gin fizz
42 Get a closer shot
43 Treeless plain
46 Guy's date
47 Moo ___ pork
50 It's a matter of personal pride
51 Inter ___ (among other things)
54 Malaria symptoms
56 Silly Putty container
57 It'll help you get started
60 Attachment to "chute" or "mount"
62 "You will ___ stranger" (psychic prediction)
63 Adam's original home
64 Kin of "By Jove!"
65 Civil Rights gp. since 1909
66 Debussy's "Clair de ___"
67 Showroom model
68 Egyptian crosses
69 Word with "rumble" or "bucket"

DOWN

1 Oilman's boon
2 Toward the beach
3 Place for a tempest
4 Bordered
5 List from a waiter
6 Hard outer covering of a seed
7 Belarus capital
8 Flip ___ (decide randomly)
9 Planned Parenthood founder Margaret
10 Explosive initials
11 "The Snake Charmer" painter
12 Originally
13 Easily annoyed
21 Atomic physicist Enrico
22 Formerly, in newspaper announcements
29 "You bet!"
30 1998 animated bug film

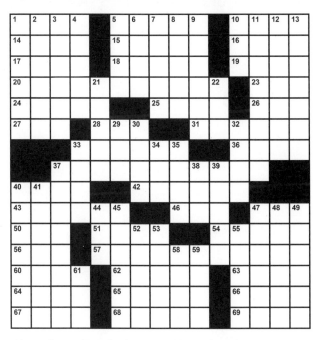

32 ___-skin cap (Davy Crockett's hat)

33 ___ out a living (barely got by)

34 Scooby ___ (TV cartoon dog)

35 Houston air problem

37 First baby picture, often

38 Singer Sumac

39 Purplish bloom

40 Soaked in liquid

41 Traveler's need

44 Rule, in India

45 Female graduate

47 Overpower by force

48 Montana's capital

49 Online newsgroup system

52 "See what ___?"

53 Vertical, nautically

55 Some Celts

58 ___ A Sketch (drawing toy)

59 Knocks on the door

61 ___ Annie of "Oklahoma!"

ACROSS

1 Final amt.
4 Balaam's beast
7 Vitamin-bottle initials
10 Org. that awards the Calder Cup
13 "Well, lookee here!"
14 Really evil
16 "___ won't be afraid" ("Stand By Me" lyric)
17 What a certain Slav does to ensure a bill is correct?
19 "La-la" lead-in
20 Dove shelter
21 Orange pekoe, e.g.
22 Cousteau's bailiwick
24 Knocking for a loop
26 It's been said
29 "Cat on a Hot ___ Roof"
30 Baseball arbiter
32 Puts into harmony
33 Goat or rabbit wool
35 "Beg pardon?"
36 Vegas introduction
37 Loving words in a luxury hotel?
40 Dartboard setting
42 Bad firecracker
43 Fit snugly one inside another
47 Ground corn dishes mixed with sugar and spices
49 Strong throw or golf tee
50 Miner's discovery
51 Iron, as clothes
53 Play, as a guitar
55 ___ out a living (making do)

56 Boston zone
58 Companion of faith and charity
59 Receptacle for coal
60 Perfumes for Mr. Ed?
64 Tripper's drug
65 Mediocre, as a hotel
66 Royal flush card
67 Raised-eyebrow remarks
68 Financially stable
69 Met filler
70 "___ to Joy" (Schiller)

DOWN

1 Bach composition, perhaps
2 Add at the last minute
3 Rioter's activity
4 "I get it" responses
5 Not a mainstream religion
6 Assess
7 Elephant-eating bird of folklore
8 "How stupid of me!"
9 Arrange by class
10 Boom box feature
11 Mann and Greeley
12 Woody vines (Var.)
15 All spruced up
18 D.C. figure
23 Seals around a bathtub
25 Hindu spiritual leader
27 Without slack
28 A fuel gas
31 Knight's fair lady
34 "Morning's at Seven" playwright Paul

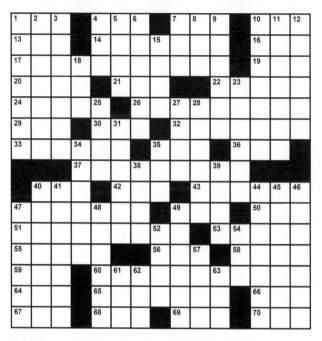

35 "I knew a man, Bojangles, and ___ dance ..."
38 Ivory-poacher's take
39 Trio for grand pianos
40 Rose-colored
41 Takes a load off
44 Capital of Ontario
45 Blew, as a volcano
46 Landed property
47 Colorado city

48 Christmastime adornments
49 Former currency of Spain
52 What we all want to pay
54 "For Whom ___ Bell Tolls"
57 Pre-1917 monarch
61 Part of IOU
62 Decay
63 Old PC monitor type

ACROSS

1 Chinese fruit with a brittle shell (Var.)
6 Duplicate
10 LP record speeds, for short
14 Athol Fugard play, "A Lesson from ___"
15 "It should come ___ surprise ..."
16 One of the Great Lakes
17 Comic character who wears no pants
19 Unit of loudness
20 Broken-down motorist's fiery signal
21 Inventor Thomas
23 Teamwork inhibitor
25 An expert in gods
28 Boorish brute
30 Mule of an old song
31 Top ten Genesis hit, "___ Deep"
32 Prince Rainier's land
35 Attention-getting sign gas
37 One choosing Canada over Vietnam
41 Sci-fi saucers
42 Mansion and grounds
45 "... ___, dust to dust"
49 Underwater vessel, briefly
51 Bustling commotions
52 Hospital suction device
56 The "I" in TGIF
57 Capitol dome
58 Archaeologist's discovery
60 Shorten manuscripts, e.g.
61 Outing for two couples
66 "... in the pot, ___ days old"
67 "___ Have Nothing"
68 Give a false impression of
69 Apparel
70 Irish Spring alternative
71 Stand for an artist

DOWN

1 Young boy
2 Worldwide workers gp.
3 Confuse or perplex
4 "Physician, ___ thyself"
5 Muslim faith
6 Military school students
7 Buckeyes' sch.
8 ___ Park (Pittsburgh Pirates' stadium)
9 Backwoods clod
10 Quit officially
11 Toast to one's health
12 Baseball's Minnie
13 Dealt with
18 Help with the dishes
22 Social page fodder
23 Freddy Krueger's street
24 Slimy stuff
26 Robber's demand
27 Substitute spread
29 La Brea goop
33 Kind of relationship
34 Light switch option
36 Written tribute
38 Reggae legend Peter
39 Seventh Greek letter

40 Extreme group
43 Day care attendee
44 Spiritual leader?
45 Upward climb
46 Moviemaking place
47 Expressing optimism
48 Acts and then some
50 Freshwater codlike fish
53 Port in southwestern Spain

54 Blanc who was the voice of Bugs Bunny
55 West Point freshman
59 Mental invention
62 Be in debt
63 Stammered syllables
64 10-10 score, e.g.
65 Electric swimmer

31 BE NICE! · By Gary Cooper

ACROSS

1 Inaugural ball, e.g.
5 Oil-producing rock
10 Heroic narrative
14 Nutmeg cover
15 Jackrabbits, actually
16 Peak of the peak
17 Re-establish relations after a rift
19 ___ Star State (Texas's nickname)
20 Georgia of "The Mary Tyler Moore Show"
21 Desertlike
22 Some pints
23 Paved, in a way
25 Ball of fire
27 Poi plant
29 Boardlike
32 Detective's assignment
35 As found
39 Suffix with "social" or "urban"
40 Romanian money unit
41 Proper behavior
42 The White House's is 20500
43 Answer incorrectly
44 Alpine crests
45 Life jacket, for one
46 Deserving of the booby prize
48 Scottish terrier
50 Bicuspid coating
54 Surgeon's stitch
58 Teenager's breakout
60 Upper pelvic bones
62 Eat, drink, and be merry

63 Foretell
64 Suspend the hostilities
66 Bistro name word
67 Reference with a world of information?
68 Alda the sitcom legend
69 Holding a grudge
70 Prognosticators
71 California winery locale

DOWN

1 Doubleheader pair
2 "You ___ kidding!"
3 Jargon of a particular field
4 How spaghetti may be cooked
5 Yonder ship
6 Fictional skater Brinker
7 Formed a curve
8 Not fully trusting
9 City in the Ruhr area
10 A hero may have it
11 Eat humble pie
12 Part of a chromosome
13 Forest hackers
18 Target of some collars
24 Moisture remover
26 Calla lily's plant family
28 Without repetition
30 "How sweet ___!"
31 Pt. of NYPD
32 Ball of thread or yarn
33 Prefix with "dynamic"
34 Capitulate
36 One off the wagon

62

37 Angry states
38 Warthog features
41 Input for a computer program
45 Experienced person
47 "Bless you" preceder
49 Circular, domed tent
51 Thin-layered minerals
52 Make giddy
53 Birthplace of Charles De Gaulle

55 Soft palate feature
56 Condensed anecdote
57 "Maria ___" (Dorsey hit)
58 "Sesame Street" teaching
59 Pacific salmon
61 One-time orchard spray
65 Beast of burden

ACROSS

1 Bird in a cornfield
5 Naked, as a sheep
10 Help a hustler
14 Goddess of youth
15 Salk vaccine target
16 Thousand-plus-pager
17 Tempt fate
20 Settle once and for all
21 Merry month
22 Baldfaced ___
23 Frowned-upon feminizing suffix
24 Dish-shaped gong
27 Uses the "+" function
29 Deeply held belief
32 Turkish commander
33 Sixth sense letters
36 Halos
38 Beachwear for men
41 Bottom line
42 Paintings and such
43 Space ball?
44 Come to a point
46 Clumsy ones
50 Outdoes
52 Geologic time division
55 Mooch, as a ride
56 Yankee great Gehrig
57 Small tobacco product
60 Goal of a blitz
63 "Well, ___ that special!"
64 See-through fabric
65 Fishing decoy
66 Connect the ___ (kid's game)
67 Church niches
68 Airport guesses, for short

DOWN

1 Spiny cactus
2 Made good on, as a loan
3 Complied with commands
4 Hit the road
5 Practices with another boxer
6 "I'm not kidding!"
7 Auto maker Ransom E. ___
8 Warden's fear
9 "... ___ gloom of night ..."
10 Black tea from India
11 "Goo goo ga ga," e.g.
12 Kind of trip for the conceited
13 IRS concern
18 "The Murders in the Rue Morgue" writer
19 Not yet a pro
24 ___ cotta
25 Grows older
26 Pas' partners
28 Small paving stone
30 Apollo 11 module
31 Pecan, e.g.
34 Heavy track item
35 Breads served with hummus
37 Catch ___ (start to understand)
38 Hamilton's dueling opponent
39 Moving about
40 Velvet pile
41 Booze abuser

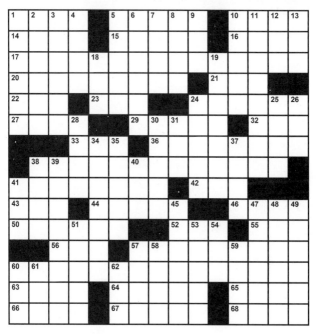

45 Lavishly entertain
47 Vowel change in related words
48 Seesaw supports
49 Has a few of 57-Across
51 Sahl and Drucker
53 Daytona 500 events
54 Noah's vessel
57 Farm yield
58 Sacred Nile bird

59 Last word in Gilligan's theme
60 Four times a day, on an Rx
61 GI show sponsor
62 ___ Peron, Argentine first lady

ACROSS

1 "Those ___ the Days"
5 English Derby site
10 Unsophisticated person
14 Islamic prayer leader
15 Back bones
16 Taro corm
17 Milk-Bone product
19 Ending for "theater" or "church"
20 It gives a tire its grip
21 Timber-to-be
22 Brought to maturity
23 Aromatic herb of the mint family
25 Parade features
27 Sharp blow
29 ___ corgi (dog breed)
32 "My Fair ___"
35 Ax at a rock concert
39 Arctic surface
40 Beatle's widow
41 Reason to be shunned, in the Bible
42 Airplane Flying Handbook org.
43 Become impeded (with "down")
44 Give the green light
45 AK or HI, once
46 "An ___ of the People" (Ibsen)
48 Paper-and-string flier
50 A 747 has two of these
54 Bantu language (Var.)
58 ___ and crafts
60 They give people big heads
62 "Above the fruited ___ ..."
63 Alpine skier Miller
64 Barking rodent?
66 Unexciting party guest
67 "Waiting to Exhale" novelist McMillan
68 Supports
69 Uptight
70 Totally befuddled
71 Worry

DOWN

1 Thickness
2 Atlanta research university
3 Foams at the mouth
4 Attache's milieu
5 Superman's emblem
6 Warsaw ___ (defense group)
7 Thin flakes from the skin
8 A college at Oxford
9 California's San ___
10 Annul
11 Miserably unhappy existence
12 ___ fixe (obsessive thought)
13 "Clear and Present Danger" star
18 Deity representation
24 They're turned by scholars
26 Not as planned
28 Most of the 101 Dalmatians
30 Surgery souvenir
31 Take, as oral arguments
32 Ear part
33 "Author unknown" byline

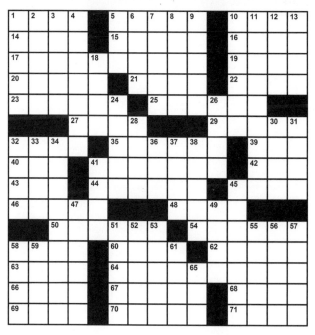

34 Cutthroat
36 Feeling of fury
37 "Honky ___ Women"
38 About in the morning
41 "Betcha can't eat just one" chips
45 Item read by a fortuneteller
47 Lover of company?
49 Amazon native
51 Greek penny

52 Plumed avian in Florida
53 Ascends dramatically
55 Anagram for "drain"
56 The "D" in LED
57 "The Scream" evocation
58 Actress Lane of old TV
59 Forty square rods
61 What to call a king
65 Deep-pile Scandinavian rug

ACROSS

1 Increase by
4 Kindergarten adhesive
9 Genesis tower
14 Turn right, to a horse
15 Anesthetic of old
16 Partner of beyond
17 Andy's doll mate
18 Rotates with a buzz
19 Turned sharply
20 Provider of rational advice
23 Hillary conquered it
24 Soup letter
27 Holding a grudge
28 Little dog sounds
31 It often contains lots of letters
32 Forster's "Howards ___"
35 Brightly colored amphibian
37 Sleep phase, for short
38 Say what you will
41 Fire remains
43 Kuwait boss
44 Norma Webster's middle name
45 Book jacket blurbs
47 Purim time
49 Exclamation of resignation
53 Early spring bloomer
55 President's concern
58 Be rude in a debate
61 Bucking horse, informally
63 Assembly line setting
64 Invitation to a visitor
65 Type of angle
66 Fuse
67 Seventh Greek letter
68 Mythical woodland deity
69 More rational
70 Brass in the Clinton White House?

DOWN

1 Century plants
2 From the beginning
3 Disputant
4 Small flycatcher
5 One of the Musketeers
6 Sly
7 Yukon or Northwest, for short
8 Hebrides language
9 Low man in the opera
10 In full flower
11 Line between two cities
12 Mother of all matriarchs
13 Spearheaded
21 Inch along
22 Reply
25 Perjury offense
26 Street of cinematic horrors
29 Prefix with "structure"
30 For each
33 Born, on the society pages
34 Patterned linen cloth
36 Lipton product
38 O.K. Corral event
39 Little goat
40 Inclined
41 Fox alternative

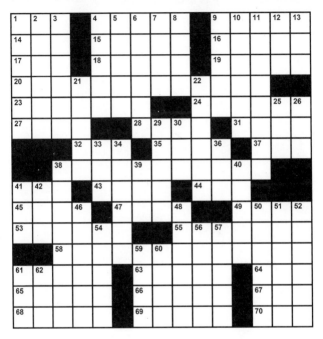

42 McCartney's title
46 Hardly plentiful
48 Keep possession of
50 No-goodniks
51 Hindu drink of the gods
52 Grammar class subject
54 Painful stomach problem
56 Richard of "The Godfather"
57 More frequently, to bards

59 "Mr. Holland's ___" (1996)
60 Bone in the arm
61 ___-relief sculpture
62 TV brand name

ACROSS

1 Rush furiously, as a river
5 Almost win, at the track
10 Crazy way to run
14 The ___ of March
15 Volcanologists study them
16 Last letter of a pilot's alphabet
17 Animal-drawn wagon
19 Banned orchard treatment
20 Pulled ___ (athlete's injury)
21 About 2.2 lbs
22 Headed out
23 Inspire love in
25 Decorative fold on a garment
27 Miscellaneous mixture
29 Less plentiful
32 They might form a circle
35 Lourdes miracle setting
39 Ended one's hunger
40 Org. in "The Bourne Identity"
41 Atomic number 75
42 Shoo-___ (likely victors)
43 He talks turkey?
44 "The only thing we have to fear is fear ___"
45 Sudden cold spell
46 Violin virtuoso Isaac
48 Citation abbreviation
50 Papal emissary
54 Forgers
58 Sighs of relief
60 Liquid butter
62 Having no drawbacks
63 ___ B'rith

64 Sound judgment
66 Cut from the same cloth
67 What a need might do
68 Neural network
69 Resurfaces a road
70 Smile in an evil way
71 Short stride

DOWN

1 Guitar fret, e.g.
2 Make pretty
3 Italian seaport
4 Inuits, e.g.
5 Tissue layer
6 Dearth
7 Benefit
8 Rhea's role in "Cheers"
9 Prevent legally
10 Star-shaped flower
11 Big hit for Frankie Laine
12 Norwegian king or saint
13 Writer Vonnegut
18 Organic compound
24 The slow lane's side
26 Dance with a king and a queen
28 They're mined and refined
30 Part of the Sicilian scenery
31 Answer (Abbr.)
32 Talent show lineup
33 Burn and loot
34 Type of fine coat
36 Number of operas composed by Beethoven
37 Bathroom floor item, often

70

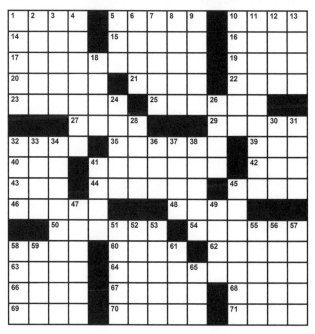

38 Small clumps
41 Boxing locale
45 Some breaking balls
47 Goo from trees
49 Parisian pals
51 Turkish officials (Var.)
52 Rose hazard
53 Like a Clive Barker novel
55 Belief

56 Waste maker of adage
57 Sheep counter's quest
58 Blind as ___
59 "You Are My Destiny" singer
61 To be, to Brutus
65 Always, poetically

IN SHAPE · By Morgan Coffey

ACROSS

1 Scratching post user
4 Coeur d'Alene's home
9 Push rudely
14 Fireplace debris
15 Blood bank fluid
16 Old Italian bread?
17 Anticipate trouble
20 Apprehenders
21 End of a tunnel, proverbially
22 Ingredients in fuzzy navels?
23 She lays around the farm
24 Instrument for a minstrel
27 WSW about-face
28 Cop's path
30 Paddler's craft
31 You may take it lying down
33 Well, just the opposite?
34 "Return to ___" (Elvis hit)
35 Like some watches
38 Andean animals
41 "Tommy" group (with "The")
42 Gullible dupes
46 Viscounts' superiors
47 Fine spray
48 Shoe-wiping spot
49 Desert of Mongolia
50 Fetched
51 Orchard Field, today
53 Royal Peruvians
55 Three-time Emmy winner Fabray
57 Provides the body with proper nourishment
60 Refrigerant trademark
61 Remove, as a brooch
62 Tiny Tim played one (Abbr.)
63 Lead-tin alloy
64 Alleviated
65 Fire engine shade

DOWN

1 23-Across, at times
2 Utterly absurd
3 King-sized furniture?
4 Castaways' homes
5 Wapiti
6 "Fine" or "liberal" followers
7 "What's that?"
8 Egg dish
9 Refinery refuse
10 Mountainous region of Scotland
11 Full-bodied, as a voice
12 The Mystery Machine, for one
13 Double-curve pipe shape
18 100 lbs. in the U.S.
19 Successfully woo
23 One who's not all there?
25 Wing-tip tip
26 Suffix with "puppet" or "profit"
28 Hindrance to fair judgment
29 Joint with a 90-degree bend
30 Not-so-great grade
32 Running back LaDainian
34 Get off ___-free
36 ___ in victory
37 Sounds of contentment

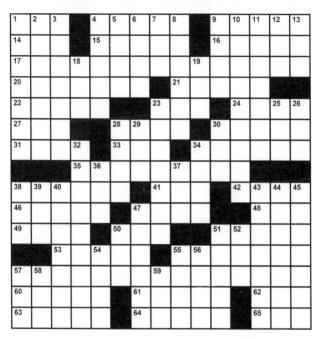

38 Tripod part
39 Doctor with seven faces
40 Umpire, for one
43 He doesn't play for pay
44 Have some
45 Girded (oneself)
47 A prayer place
50 It's dispensed from a hose
51 Upturned, as a crate

52 Be verbally evasive
54 Walker's aid
55 Kindergarten time-outs
56 "Acoustic Soul" singer India.___
57 Juvenile amphibian
58 You-here link
59 Spanish feminine article

ACROSS

1 J. Fred Muggs was one
6 Feeling feverish
9 "Gone With the Wind" star Clark
14 Defame, in a way
15 Actor Benicio ___ Toro
16 Welder's wear
17 Not merely smoldering
18 Gabor sister
19 Be moved by a stimulus
20 Upstart who makes insolent comments
23 Mike's partner on candy boxes
24 Start for "Paulo" or "Luis"
25 Embellisher
27 Calligraphy technique
32 Pertaining to the ear
33 Grier of "Foxy Brown"
34 Meddlesome woman
36 Chloroform kin
39 Certain gemstone
41 Of tender years
43 Dublin's isle
44 Nasal openings
46 Six-day race vehicles
48 ___ through your teeth
49 Kangaroo stabilizer
51 Hid from view
53 More rarely encountered
56 Whitney or Rushmore (Abbr.)
57 "2001: A Space Odyssey" mainframe
58 Memorize
64 Sherlock Holmes's friend Adler

66 Wrap with feathers
67 "Peter, Peter, pumpkin ___ ..."
68 Nut for pies
69 Dinner plate scraping
70 Less-played 45 part
71 Comedian Wanda
72 Rubble creator
73 Legendary Himalayan creatures

DOWN

1 Talon
2 Sound system, briefly
3 Wading bird in hieroglyphics
4 Most insignificant
5 Complete in every respect
6 ___ fixe (obsessive thought)
7 Strauss of blue jeans
8 Andes beast of burden
9 Inquisition choker
10 Long-armed animal
11 Creative idea
12 Eastwood's "The Gauntlet" costar
13 Put into the record
21 "Nonsense!"
22 Tokyo, formerly
26 Religious ceremony
27 "___ further review ..."
28 ___ John's (pizza chain)
29 Sassy sort
30 Revolving door's lack
31 Vanity cases
35 Sacred Egyptian cross
37 Lake or city

74

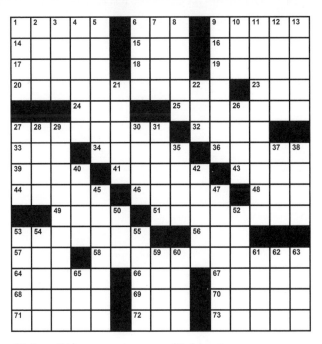

38 Rex or Walter
40 "The Jeffersons" writer Norman
42 Hardly sterile
45 Repulses
47 Auction house namesake
50 Gridiron great Dawson
52 Restless feeling
53 They may pass in the night
54 "I Still Believe" singer Mariah

55 Automaton
59 Slightly tattered
60 Matted cotton for stuffing
61 "Look ___ this way ..."
62 Quick, in some product names
63 Number between dos and cuatro
65 No, in Scotland

ACROSS

1 Western projectile
6 Sammy of the Cubs
10 "Beetle Bailey" bulldog
14 Addition to a building
15 ___ about (approximately)
16 Lose one's grip on
17 Two desserts in one
19 Moore of "Ghost"
20 Spanish girlfriend
21 "Shogun" sequel
23 "Iron Chef" prop
25 Place with a lot of heat?
28 Footnote abbr.
30 Bull ___ china shop
31 Where fathers may gather
32 Saintly Mother
35 Word preceding "circus" and "market"
37 Accurately representing the real world
41 AK or HI, once
42 Very fair, as hair
45 Cop ___ (bargain with the DA)
49 Physicians' org.
51 View from a pew
52 Advancement
56 ___ out (withdraw)
57 San Simeon castle builder
58 A Yorkshire city
60 "Oh, woe ___!"
61 Elite, familiarly
66 Two in the middle of "middle"
67 Promgoer's need

68 Measure at the jeweler's
69 Norms (Abbr.)
70 Distinctive style
71 Gradually expand

DOWN

1 Pass again in a race
2 "Little Plastic Castle" singer DiFranco
3 Gym shoes
4 A clothes-knit union?
5 Flower of the primrose family
6 From Mogadishu
7 Bed-in for peace participant Yoko
8 Roll-on lawn
9 Craggy ridge
10 Strange thing
11 Mine shaft drill
12 Club sandwich vegetable
13 Expressed one's beliefs
18 Years ___ (in the past)
22 Attack
23 Ad-libber's asset
24 "___ to Joy" (Schiller)
26 Rats, so to speak
27 Baby beluga
29 "Apocalypto" director Gibson
33 Indian instruments
34 Top of a suit?
36 Sleigh filler, once a year
38 Depression and Prohibition, for two
39 Govt. air-safety org.
40 Cause of frostbite or suntan

43 Uncommon sense?
44 It's for those who get butterflies
45 Plant attackers
46 Adjusted beforehand
47 Covered with rich soil
48 It gives you an out
50 "Annie" actress Quinn
53 Chopin composition
54 Contraction in "The Star-Spangled Banner"

55 Head-shoulder connectors
59 Command to a Western gunslinger
62 Chum
63 School open-house organizer
64 Mineo of movies
65 Sum (Abbr.)

ACROSS

1 Grasped
5 ___-bodied
9 Affected by ennui
14 Margarine
15 Unimagined
16 French place of learning
17 Where Muscat is capital
18 Enjoys gourmet entrees
19 Gathers
20 Canadian comedy troupe (with "The")
23 Swiss canton
24 Shape of St. Anthony's Cross
25 "I was at my girlfriend's at the time," and others
28 Bamboo-eating animal
30 Song of David
33 "And now, without further ___ ..."
34 "It's still the same ___ story"
36 Winter time on Cape Cod
37 Applied frosting
38 Raymond Chandler whodunit (with "The")
42 Chanel of perfume
43 Prefix with "duct"
44 Wide-turning vehicle
45 What rock fans may dig?
46 "Dances With Wolves" structure
48 Rose-colored dye
52 White-knuckle emotion
54 Horse unlikely to win a race
56 Hot air can inflate it?
57 Play by Matt Crowley (with "The")
61 Pay to persuade
63 Burned up the road
64 Yanks' third baseman, familiarly
65 Word with "space" or "limits"
66 Bivalve mollusk
67 Real estate measure
68 Yawning gap
69 Apes kangaroos
70 Tool repository

DOWN

1 Connect, as a stereo
2 New York city where Mark Twain is buried
3 Opening bars
4 Crime family heads
5 Where Kings may go to beat the Heat
6 The worse for wear
7 Backing for plaster
8 Something ___ (extraordinary)
9 "Don't panic!"
10 Eyelike windows
11 Reduce prices
12 Ninety-degree wing
13 ___ Plaines, Ill.
21 "Boot" in the Mediterranean
22 Shoulder-baring top
26 ___ fixe (obsession)
27 Covering for a outdoor bald spot
29 Extinct bird that couldn't fly
31 Hairs on a caterpillar, e.g.

32 Word with "blond" or "Wednesday"
35 Wetsuit wearers
37 "Othello" antagonist
38 Folktales and such
39 Sourness
40 Small drink of liquor
41 Belgian city
42 Bedroll alternative
46 Cats, with yarn or mice
47 Catch in a snare

49 Manhunt
50 Give the cold shoulder to
51 Signaled assent
53 Court attire
55 "Pardon me" grunts
58 Cast wearer's frustration
59 ___ contendere (court plea)
60 Bighorn bleats
61 Tropical snake
62 "... ay, there's the ___"

ACROSS

1 Fond du ___, Wisc.
4 United voting group
8 Motorist's stopover
13 United Nations agcy.
14 Eater of eucalyptus leaves
15 Bring forth, as an emotion
16 Bargain container
17 Diameters halved
18 Palindromic belief
19 The police might do this
22 It has a negative charge
23 Artist Yoko
24 "Little Red Book" chairman
27 Changes a B to an A-
31 Where the worldly-wise have been
33 Money in Japan
34 "Thanks ___!"
36 Sundance entry, often
37 Repairs damaged relations
41 Employee of a dictator?
43 "... ___ cost to you"
44 Fleur-de-___ (Quebec symbol)
47 Merchandise at a white sale
49 It's burned on the road
52 Up to now
53 Vietnamese city
55 ___ Rosa, Calif.
56 Make new contacts
60 Divest of weapons
63 Careful shopper's criterion
64 "Of Thee I Sing" lyricist Gershwin
65 Neighbor of Lebanon and Iraq
66 Prince of the Middle East (Var.)
67 Zero, to Nero
68 Respond to, as a tip
69 Patches things up?
70 Clock-setting standard (Abbr.)

DOWN

1 Place for many books
2 Certain title holder
3 Type of shop with second-hand goods
4 Wild swine
5 Fill with cargo
6 Musical miscellany
7 Africa's largest capital city
8 Markedly rapid
9 Walkie-talkie word
10 Won ___ soup
11 ___ out a living (barely get by)
12 Serve that doesn't count
14 Swedish monetary unit
20 Rocky crag
21 It must be in the genes
24 Negative campaigning
25 Taking it away makes a maid mad?
26 Written tribute
28 The old man
29 "Born Free" beast
30 Sound heard twice in "George"
32 ___-eyed jack
35 Unusually narrow shoe size
38 180 deg. from WSW

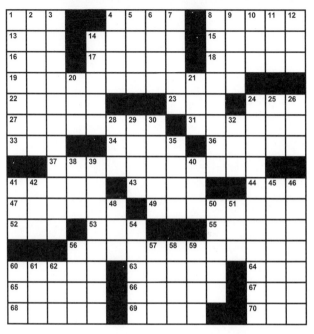

39 Like creatures from outer space
40 Tel. book contents
41 Clandestine and canny
42 Common Father's Day gift
45 Time gap
46 Ocean condiment
48 ___ juris (in one's own right)
50 Basketry willow
51 Young boy

54 Shoemaker's helpers, in a fairy tale
56 Liveliness
57 Title for Agatha Christie
58 Exploded, as a tire
59 Feels repentant
60 Made in the ___
61 Big Apple inits.
62 Exhibited matter

ACROSS

1 "As You Like It" character
6 Maestro's concern
11 Egyptian god of the air
14 "___ you glad you did?"
15 Prior to, in the backwoods
16 Number of fugitives on a noted list
17 Substitute at the plate
19 Come to a conclusion
20 Store, as fodder
21 "Just a ___!" ("Hold on!")
22 Walking aid
23 Repairs with thread
25 Like figureheads
27 A glutton has a big one
31 ___ spell (took a load off)
32 Milk maker's call
33 "National Velvet" writer Bagnold
34 Harley rider
37 Persian Gulf country
39 Beetles-to-be
42 Thatching palm
43 Come up again and again
45 Henhouse
47 Word between "game" and "match"
48 Makes a quick retreat
50 Ways to leave
52 Peevish
55 "Now hold on there!"
56 Prospector's find
57 Zadora of "Butterfly"
59 City near Syracuse
63 Lincoln's sobriquet
64 Help somewhat
66 Tractor-trailer combo
67 On ___-to-know basis
68 Place for a French lesson
69 Conjoined twin name
70 Rosie of "Do the Right Thing"
71 Ecological sequences

DOWN

1 Superhero's accessory
2 Home of Aer Lingus
3 Periscope part
4 Cut with a scalpel
5 Wheaties box candidate
6 ___ chi (Chinese martial art)
7 Terrestrial amphibians
8 Church choral work
9 Concise summary
10 Atop, poetically
11 Run after the buss?
12 Reddish dye
13 Below the surface
18 Doing a hatchet job
22 Interrupt, as a dancer
24 Wield a spoon
26 It's run up and then settled
27 Middle Eastern chief (Var.)
28 You sweat through it
29 Certain cooked breakfast item
30 Bring out
35 Sport with swords
36 "Willard" creatures
38 Almost, but not ___

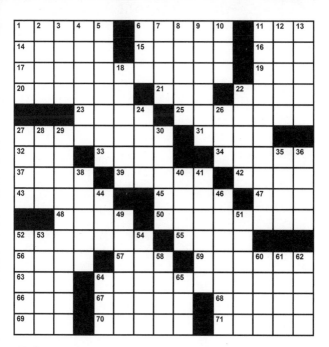

40 Peat sources
41 Somewhat
44 Wrestling official (Abbr.)
46 State symbols of Indiana
49 On one's back
51 "King of Queens" character
52 Disabled vehicle alert
53 Red-breasted songbird
54 Prisoner who'll never get out

58 Fit to ___
60 Transylvanian lab assistant
61 Remove, to an editor
62 War god
64 Indy measure
65 Curved carpenter's tool

ACROSS

1 Cash alternative
6 Get behind
10 Mimic a kangaroo
14 Printer's proof, for short
15 Part of A.A. Milne
16 Sicilian hot spot
17 Tire feature
18 Warm-hearted
19 Short-lived, charged lepton
20 Irrelevant
23 Start for "Tome" or "Tiago"
24 Distinctive flair
25 Elephant carrier of myth
28 Terror group in "Mississippi Burning"
31 Weightlifting maneuver
35 Poet's "black"
37 Abel's nephew
39 Boise's home
40 Out of public view
43 Daughter of Spain's King Juan Carlos
44 Itty-bitty bit
45 Three-player game
46 The film industry
48 Stupidly bad, in slang
50 Place for a facial
51 Scout's shelter
53 Ribosomal ___
55 Poker long shot
62 Opposite of "yep"
63 Celebrated clinic
64 Refrigerator coolant
66 Run in the Hambletonian
67 Ruffles
68 Frighteningly strange
69 This answer is a four-letter word
70 Where to find some tars
71 Passed out on the poker table?

DOWN

1 Monitor type, for short
2 Ginseng, e.g.
3 Dueling sword
4 Lacking refinement
5 Type of bear
6 Cause of misery
7 Touched the tarmac
8 Where the loot gets left
9 Prepares to be knighted
10 Some citrus drinks
11 Fancy sewing case
12 Shortly, to Shakespeare
13 Cool off like a collie
21 Rationed (out)
22 Word with "button" or "room"
25 Renaissance stringed instrument
26 Old manuscript markings
27 Borat portrayer
29 Opposing voice
30 "When pigs fly!"
32 Vehicles with caterpillar treads
33 Penny-pinching
34 Popular ground cover plant
36 Notable birthday
38 Words before "precedent"

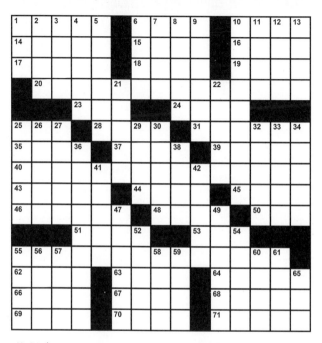

41 No longer anonymous
42 Wedge-shaped bones
47 Iron-poor blood condition
49 Stabbed with a stiletto
52 Crowned heads of old
54 What nouns and verbs must do
55 "Come ___ my parlor ..."
56 Author Ephron
57 Dick and Jane's dog

58 Little fellow
59 Civil rights activist Parks
60 Zeus's wife and sister
61 Work like a dog
65 Type of earnings or income

ACROSS

1. Cliffs
6. "You're it!" game
9. Couldn't hide one's astonishment
14. Bright prospect
15. "To ___ is human"
16. Dunne of "I Remember Mama"
17. Petroleum company
18. Pasture
19. Be a coquette
20. Post-Iditarod dessert?
23. Bossy's chew
24. Ask payment
25. Inexact recipe amounts
27. Wide-ranging, as tastes
32. All-nighter site, perhaps
33. Miss Piggy's "me"
34. Ten percent church donation
36. Protracted attack
39. "___ la Douce"
41. "It ___ to me that ..."
43. Become fuzzy
44. "The Canterbury Tales" character
46. Big pipes
48. Victoria's Secret purchase
49. Weigh-station stopper
51. Achievement levels
53. Late October zodiac sign
56. Partner of games
57. Patch pitch
58. Novelist Anne's favorite dessert?
64. Charge, as with feeling
66. "___ he drove out of sight ..."
67. Author who worked on Friday?
68. Onionlike vegetables
69. Zebra kin
70. Art-studio fixture
71. Bags at the mall
72. It's usually less than gross?
73. Metallic waste product

DOWN

1. Labor union foe
2. 1977 best-seller set at Boston Memorial Hospital
3. A bad way to run
4. A hairline may do it
5. Result of multiplying
6. "___ it to the judge"
7. Math student's calculation, sometimes
8. Catch on
9. Romani people in Spain
10. "Blessed ___ the meek ..."
11. Dessert that makes one feel warm and toasty?
12. Follow afterward
13. Some safety deposit box documents
21. Thumbs-down group
22. Young goat
26. Babe's bed
27. Abu Dhabi prince
28. Apple center
29. Dessert that makes one green with envy?
30. Agenda listing
31. "Talk is ___"

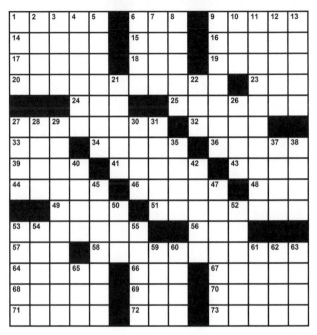

35 Olympic track champion Zatopek
37 Wise mentor
38 Periods of history on a timeline
40 State with confidence
42 More than just a mistake
45 Catherine the Great was one
47 Like some collars or tires
50 "East" on a grandfather clock
52 Create warm feelings for

53 Basketball legend Wilt the ___
54 A bit more than a walk-on
55 Pacific, for one
59 Celtic tongue
60 Bug you want to swat
61 "Assuming that's true ..."
62 Disappointing RSVPs
63 Mousse relatives
65 "Aloha 'Oe" instrument, briefly

ACROSS

1 Create a lasting impression?
5 Brooklet
9 Disney classic
14 100 centesimi
15 Decorative needle case
16 Hang trimmings on
17 Memory, in a film
19 Plant of the water lily family
20 Spiced Starbucks beverage
21 Slangy affirmatives
23 "I cannot tell a ___"
24 Be inquisitive
26 Lupino of "High Sierra"
28 Requiring the least driving
30 Quality affecting taste
32 Is compelled to
34 "When Irish ___ are smiling ..."
35 Desert stinger
37 Conditional conjunctions
39 Nickname for one who is light on his feet
42 Participant in some receptions
43 Said over
46 What a soldier shouldn't be
49 Extremely small amount
51 Fence crossing
52 Dramatic scene
54 Asian tongue
56 Wrestling finale
57 Architectural annex
58 Pt. of MIT
60 Front part of plane
62 A way to think
64 Quirky joint
68 Vague perception
69 Gutter holder
70 Arabian gulf
71 Tarzan creator's first name
72 Bakery offerings
73 Disapproving clucks

DOWN

1 Toymaker of myth
2 "... ___ the cows come home"
3 Far-fetched, as an idea
4 "Slung" dish
5 Keep an auction going
6 Call ___ night
7 "Peanuts" character
8 Claims similarities
9 Cork substitute
10 Excited activity
11 Multi-colored garment of a jester
12 Discolored injury
13 Alaska and Hawaii on U.S. maps, often
18 Sharp, as a turn
22 Bantam
24 Jenny or jack
25 Body bag?
27 Run ___ (go berserk)
29 Find another table for
31 "1984" author
33 Affording no illumination
36 Like Bollywood
38 Desolated

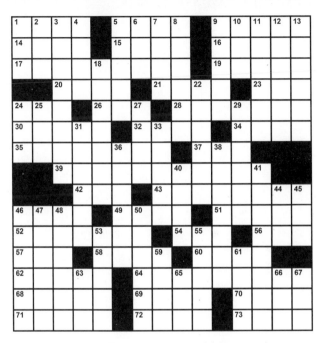

40 Abbreviated catchall
41 Fellows may receive them
44 Quarterback Manning
45 Place for a Barcalounger, perhaps
46 Words that affect one's standing?
47 Fortified, in a way
48 Watermelon-shaped
50 Forced removal from office

53 Bird that gets you down
55 Suffix with "attend" or "appear"
59 Breakfast-in-bed facilitator
61 Three-handed card game
63 Neighbor to Can.
65 "Now ___ seen everything!"
66 Cry while jumping on a chair
67 Tennis doubles?

ACROSS

1 Storage room
6 Alpha, ___, gamma
10 Charges for admission
14 Sound of a perfect basketball shot
15 Middle East gulf
16 Way out sign
17 Wrestling maneuver
19 Editor's removal mark
20 Much of Mississippi?
21 Owl, by nature
23 Hailed vehicle
25 TV, compared to a movie theater
28 Red sign's word
30 Bovine sound
31 Comes by honestly
32 Sean Penn movie
35 Work too hard
37 Like police vests
41 Performer "trapped" in a box
42 Declare to be true
45 North Dakota city
49 Robinson or Doubtfire
51 Cook a pizza
52 Being a bad guest, in a way
56 Get ___ of (eliminate)
57 Per ___ (for each person)
58 Harvests
60 Ollie's partner in slapstick
61 Air show maneuver
66 ___ back (relaxed)
67 Double-curved molding
68 "We ___ please!"
69 Misspeaks, e.g.
70 Traveled by horseback or bus
71 Shabby, as a motel

DOWN

1 Bonfire remnant
2 Pan Am rival, once
3 Something just waiting to go off
4 Credos
5 Game with 16 men on a side
6 Christmas tree choice
7 Old name of Japan's capital
8 Private eye, slangily
9 Egyptian symbols of life
10 Brimmed hat
11 English prep school town
12 Brennan of "The Sting"
13 Stems' opposites
18 Dream-sleep acronym
22 Endangered wildcat
23 Hit forensics series on CBS
24 "... one leg ___ time"
26 Scratch-off game, e.g.
27 Part of a shoelace knot
29 Nittany Lions sch.
33 "Close, but no cigar"
34 1051, on a monument
36 Tax-deferred savings plan
38 Austen's Woodhouse
39 Wagering site in NYC
40 Intimidating
43 Enjoy a snowy slope

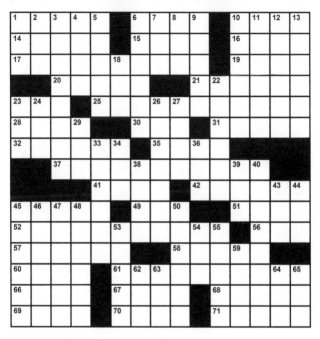

44 Williams the baseball legend
45 Bo's'n's quarters
46 James Cameron's blockbuster film
47 What mechanics do
48 Uses a coffee mill
50 "Yes ___, Bob!"
53 Small drum accompanying a fife
54 Maiden name indicator

55 Fancy parties
59 ___-dieu (kneeling bench)
62 "... long, long ___"
63 Wine suggestion
64 Abbr. at the end of some business names
65 Myrna of old movies

ACROSS

1 Person with a puffy white hat
5 Adhesive
10 "Back to the Future" destination
14 Zeus's sister and spouse
15 They're above sea level
16 Distinctive style
17 Is neither late nor early
20 Undeniable facts
21 The night before Christmas, e.g.
22 "Sesame Street" watcher
23 Mas' men
24 Pastors and priests
27 Zipper alternative
29 Standard of perfection
32 ___ West (inflatable life jacket)
33 Aussie bird
36 Airport area
38 Last straw
41 Seuss's Horton, for one
42 Place to spend the night
43 Drink daintily
44 Not on the level
46 Where the sun rises
50 7 Up alternative
52 Blow away, so to speak
55 "For Whom ___ Bell Tolls"
56 Suffix with "organ" or "patriot"
57 National cemetery on the Potomac
60 Conception to delivery
63 Word with "history" or "hygiene"
64 Excessive, as force

65 "Fifteen Miles on the ___ Canal"
66 "Get rid of it," to a proofreader
67 Arrests, in slang
68 ___ one's way (proceed along)

DOWN

1 Pies in the boardroom
2 Immediately afterward, in legalese
3 "Oops!" list, in publishing
4 Flunk out
5 Michelangelo's 1499 marble masterpiece
6 St. Francis's city
7 Blackthorn fruit
8 Bills with Hamilton's portrait
9 Suffix that maximizes
10 Pet ___ (annoyance)
11 City official
12 ___ Paulo
13 You can have a blast with it
18 Red carpet walker
19 Rowdy one
24 Bones affected by typing
25 "Atlas Shrugged" character
26 "That's an affirmative"
28 Chick's chirp
30 "The Divine Comedy" penner
31 A little bit of work
34 Title for Gandhi
35 Authoritative proclamation
37 Botanical climber
38 It might be on one's radar

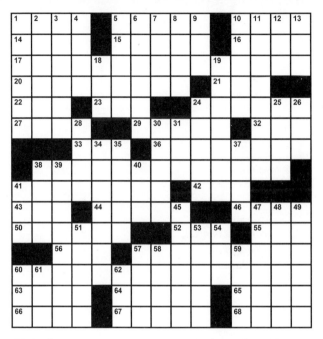

39 Retaliation

40 Writing fluid

41 Superman's emblem

45 Brownie mix-in

47 Apparel

48 Certain victor

49 Watched over, as a bar

51 Tough fiber for baskets

53 Cleans up a spill

54 180 degrees from WSW

57 Japanese native

58 There are 320 in a mile

59 Got taller

60 In ___ we trust

61 "... ___ he drove out of sight ..."

62 Bath vessel

ACROSS

1 Old orchard spray
5 Per ___ (by the day)
9 Trim a steak, for example
14 Rankle
15 U2's land, to its natives
16 Susan Lucci role on "All My Children"
17 Truce
19 Solitary one
20 1970s dance craze
21 ___-frutti (ice cream flavor)
23 Windmill blade
26 Creaks and squeaks in the night
29 Anatomy class teaching aid
33 With opulence
34 Glass squares
35 Sedately dignified
37 PC-linking system
38 Emulate Miss Daisy
39 Human or alien
40 Late percussion great Puente
41 Reptile on the Nile
42 Try a bite
43 Used picks on a vein
44 Anxiety
46 Indolence
48 Oft-pulled areas for athletes
49 "___ go bragh!"
50 One who gives blood
52 Evidence of rain
57 Immature egg, to a zoologist
59 Conks out suddenly

62 Potato preparation aid
63 Transport for Tarzan
64 ___ mater
65 Cotton sheets
66 Kind of group or pressure
67 Primordial substance

DOWN

1 Symbol of St. Louis
2 In ___ of (standing in for)
3 Woeful exclamation
4 Take a break
5 Overcome in battle
6 Three, on a sundial
7 Write down the wrong answer, e.g.
8 Wrestling contest
9 Shoulder muscle
10 Like the Kama Sutra
11 Marathoner's destination
12 Top of a card suit
13 Surfacing gunk
18 Legendary toy makers
22 Strip of gear, as a ship
24 Mr. Potato Head parts
25 Give the right, as to privileges
27 Makes joyful
28 Ecclesiastical districts
29 Bounded
30 Type of deli roll
31 Final version
32 Jeans brand
36 Bend ___ (listen attentively)
39 Low man in the chorus

40 Type of plate or soldier
42 Sawbucks
43 Calculator symbol
45 Shrinking flower?
47 Sleeping bag closure
51 Answer an invitation
53 June 6, 1944 remembrance
54 Farmer's place, in a song
55 Feeble, as an excuse

56 Cheese tray item
57 Sun or moon, poetically
58 By way of
60 "___ a yellow ribbon ..."
61 Bill featuring Washington

ACROSS

1 Broadway's "___ Mia!"
6 Canter's cousin
10 "Faster ___ a speeding bullet"
14 Sign that's often lit
15 Poet's jet black
16 Clearly in good health
17 In dire need
19 "What ___ is new?"
20 Dress regally
21 Skyscraper transport
23 Annoy but good
25 See 6-Across
26 Leg, to a film noir detective
29 "Take ___ song and make it better" (Beatles lyric)
31 Satellite radio giant
35 "___ as directed"
36 Suffix with "psych"
38 Crinkly gauze fabric
39 "Beats me"
43 Bristlelike parts
44 Grain storage site
45 See 23-Across
46 Make certain
48 Pub hardware
50 End-of-letter letters
51 Soprano Jenny, the "Swedish Nightingale"
53 Waterways through South America
55 "Desperate Housewives" lane
59 Ridge with a gentle slope on one side
63 "No" voter

64 Not in the neighborhood, say
66 Supermarket checkout action
67 Made a right turn
68 Guiding philosophy
69 Install, as drapes
70 Gael's language
71 Blackmore heroine Lorna

DOWN

1 A la ___ (with ice cream)
2 Prolific unknown author?
3 Bryn ___ College
4 Underage one
5 Desert peninsula
6 Was in first place
7 Symphony instrument
8 Young chicken, partridge, or turkey
9 Walks on stage
10 Flamboyantly overdone
11 Sentry's "stop!"
12 By the same token
13 "... ___ the twain shall meet"
18 Willie of country music
22 Exclamation at an unveiling
24 Certain bridge positions
26 Pretext
27 White with fright
28 Vegan's no-nos
30 Finger or toe
32 Long Island airport location
33 Seize illegally
34 Searches for
37 Kind of panel or power

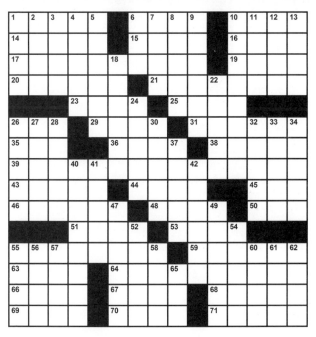

40 Bounding vigorously
41 Supernaturally strange
42 They're debatable
47 Make one's blood boil
49 Pickled
52 Cube creator, in the kitchen
54 Barroom brawl, e.g.
55 It dries on the line
56 Native of old Peru

57 ___ "the Man" Musial
58 Greek war god
60 NY gallery district
61 Minnesota ballplayer
62 "Utter" conclusion
65 Praiseful poem

ARE YOU READY FOR SOME FOOTBALL? ·
By Henry Quarters

ACROSS

1 Equal share for two
5 Ancient literary work
9 Sneaker bottom
14 "The African Queen" scriptwriter
15 Tidily organized
16 Rhythmic Cuban dance
17 Prescribed amount
18 Unload stress
19 Blue book test answer
20 Without any meaningful motive
23 "What was ___ think?"
24 Fleur-de-___
25 Flowery cake garnish
29 From that moment on
31 Quick on the uptake
33 "___ we having fun yet?"
34 Alternative passage in music
36 Made from fleece
39 Collection of lures and hooks
42 Metrical foot
43 Cake tier
44 Mine metal
45 Part of a checklist
47 Sooner's alternative
51 Monastery lodging
54 Pen ___ (letter-writing friend)
56 Words before "king" or "mode"
57 Emergency determination
60 Water-loving nymph
63 Earthy color
64 Grand in scope

65 Garlic-flavored mayonnaise
66 Happily-after link
67 Cuban monetary unit
68 Fountain pen feather
69 A or B, on a cassette
70 Row in a bowl

DOWN

1 Pilgrims to Mecca (Var.)
2 Rabbit-sized rodent
3 It may be written on a chalkboard
4 They have arches
5 Poem's final stanza (Var.)
6 Moccasin material
7 Cold and damp, as a basement
8 Apparel
9 Long journeys
10 Charlotte ___ (cream-filled dessert)
11 Typesetter's measures
12 Org. many lawyers belong to
13 One of seven per week
21 Packed with pulp
22 Tim of "The Carol Burnett Show"
26 Six-foot-eight, for example
27 Apple or pear producer
28 Nighttime, in poetry
30 The bottom line, to a consumer
32 Sharp-eyed bird of prey
35 Glassmaker's material
37 Spots on peacock feathers
38 Pod used in gumbo

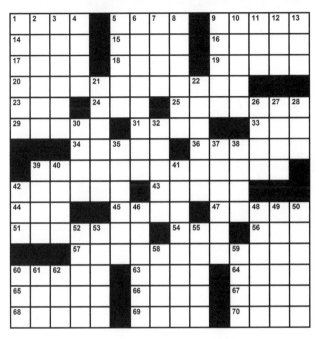

39 Card game in some casinos
40 Treats, as a sprain
41 Meddled
42 Homer Simpson exclamation
46 Cheyenne shelters
48 Taiwan's capital
49 Girl who lives in the Plaza Hotel
50 Bitter resentment

52 One of 150 in the Old Testament
53 Sundance Film Festival entry
55 Thing lacking for the common cold
58 606, to the Romans
59 Thirty-day mo.
60 Toddler's midday break
61 Be unwell
62 "Promise to pay" letters

50 | TOO SPICY FOR YOU? · By Gary Cooper

ACROSS

1 It's often removed from shrimp
5 Cousins of mandolins
10 As many as
14 ___ mater
15 It may be watched with binoculars
16 Slender-billed sea bird
17 Spicy Robert Burns poem?
20 Big fans
21 Time period
22 Word with "hang" or "take"
23 Toothpaste variety
24 Puts on at least one coat
27 Place with a very tricky serpent
29 Bumper sticker
32 Louse-to-be
33 Take unfair advantage of
36 Concluding movement
38 Be a spicy speeder?
41 Extended in a different direction
42 "All in favor" word
43 Rocks, to a barkeep
44 Cabby's charges
46 Uses a straw
50 Deer with three-pointed antlers
52 NBA competitor, once
55 Britain's Queen ___
56 Mo. for most Leos
57 Pleasing to the taste
60 Person growing a spicy crop?
63 Cut hair or coupons
64 Band of eight

65 Assist a cat burglar, e.g.
66 Potter's material
67 Brides' attendants
68 Wines to serve with beef

DOWN

1 Abandon a building
2 Managed to avoid
3 Unlikely to be affected
4 Ammunition for a carpenter's gun
5 Singer/actress Lenya
6 Defend against criticism
7 Okla., before 1907
8 Piccadilly statue, popularly
9 Prepared to play piano
10 Embryos' homes
11 Every year
12 Take a crack at
13 Not even a few
18 Worn-out horse
19 Good for you
24 Carb-loading dish
25 The motion of the ocean
26 ___-Foy, Quebec (Abbr.)
28 Zap in a microwave
30 Lyrical poem
31 North Atlantic catch
34 Condition of servitude
35 Samantha of "Doctor Dolittle"
37 Soapmaking substances
38 Mineral that forms in sheets
39 Rosary recital
40 " ___ the ramparts ..."

41 Affront, in street slang
45 Like most pretzels
47 Have a drink or two
48 Yanked
49 Produces steel
51 Causing jolts
53 Thailand money
54 Eroded (with "away")
57 One-sixth of an inch, in printing

58 Support withholder
59 The month following Shevat
60 Org. that fines for obscenities
61 "___ in the Family"
62 CD-___ (computer insert)

ON A PICNIC · By J.J. Meers

ACROSS

1 It concerns write wrongs?
6 Casablanca cap
9 You get bills from them
13 Historic fort in Texas
14 Citizen of Vientiane
15 Zooms upward
16 Topic that may be best avoided
18 Salad greenery
19 Russian rulers of yesteryear
20 Sajak of "Wheel of Fortune"
21 Surround, as a castle
24 Adapt musically
28 Frees from a cage
29 One million million
30 New Mexico art colony
31 Indistinct
32 ___ the line (obey)
33 Meet expectations
37 Sexless possessive
38 "His ___ on the Sparrow"
39 Mary had a little one
41 They speak first and then drink
43 Wee foot-warmer
45 City saved by Joan of Arc
46 Genesis villain
47 Stuff studied in genetics
48 Landed estate
49 French farewell
52 Between a rock and a hard place
56 Wedding announcement
57 Bewhiskered trash invader
58 Promotional gimmick

59 "The Witching Hour" author Rice
60 Fleeceable female
61 Wise men

DOWN

1 "Well, ___-di-dah!"
2 Nobel-winning U.N. agcy.
3 Vampire, in flight
4 Least forceful, as threats
5 Undo, as laces
6 Emergency light for a motorist
7 Patronizes a diner
8 Where to observe rare animals
9 Pertaining to the largest artery of the heart
10 ___ Bo (Billy Blanks's exercise system)
11 Miss, after marriage
12 Threatened snake's sound
15 Red shade
17 Price stickers
20 Toyota hybrid
21 "___ seriously folks ..."
22 Legislator, essentially
23 Type of post-divorce support
24 Hundred-eyed giant
25 Potassium ___ (saltpeter)
26 The Marines want a few
27 Detroit-to-Montreal dir.
29 Strainer made of woolen cloth
31 Takes an alternate course
34 Shot given after stepping on a nail
35 Wolflike carrion eater

36 Loss-of-hair condition
37 Most watched judge of 1995, probably
40 You might put one on a horse
42 Calm, cool, and collected
43 Audible warning on the road
44 Planetary paths
46 Roof material
48 Work on, as a bone
49 Org. that lobbies for lawyers

50 Roseanne's TV husband
51 Days on the road?
52 Feeling of fury
53 Frat party purchase
54 Make up an alibi
55 Funny pair?

ACROSS

1 "This ___" ("How strange")
6 Tax pro
9 Like many trees in winter
13 Bowler's feat
14 "___ now, brown cow?"
15 Tool for boring holes
16 Command to a scout or quarterback?
18 Drug used to treat Parkinson's disease
19 "... ___ which will live in infamy" (FDR)
20 Boozing binge
21 Crowns of victory in ancient Greece
24 "On My Own" singer Patti
28 Meteorological event
29 When tripled, a real estate mantra
30 Backgammon necessity
31 Cobra's weapon
32 Trail mix morsel
33 Halftime features, sometimes
37 Farm brooder
38 Place to find a date in the desert?
39 Where Marco Polo explored
41 One's spiritual being
43 Private pupils
45 Foils
46 Gluttons for punishment
47 Thinnish middle?
48 Ice cream dessert
49 Paying heed

52 Countdown of top tunes
56 Scottish town
57 Furious feeling
58 "Not in a million years!"
59 Cruel fellow
60 Banned insect control agent
61 "The Story of ___ H"

DOWN

1 Suffix with "lobby" or "ideal"
2 Resort feature
3 Bookshelf wood, perhaps
4 More dismal
5 Make numb
6 Debt markers
7 ___ fun at (ridicule)
8 Reverence
9 Financial report column
10 Back in time
11 Sales agent, briefly
12 Historical time
15 Mobile home?
17 Saintly headdress
20 Son of Isaac
21 Was in command
22 Comestible item
23 Beyond the ordinary
24 Hankers (for)
25 Buckingham of Fleetwood Mac
26 Crummier
27 Suffix with "respond"
29 Russian Revolution leader
31 Some charge cards
34 City of Greece

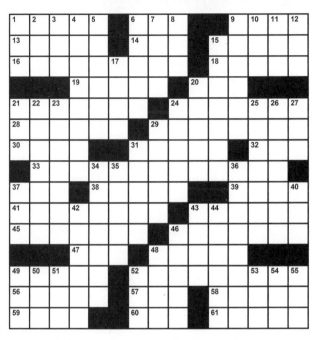

35 Parts of a harness
36 Yakked on and on
37 Towel embroidery word
40 Mule's dad
42 Come into view
43 Push down, as tobacco in a pipe
44 Illinois college town
46 Choral music composition
48 Feeder frequenter

49 Blood letters?
50 Haul
51 Miscalculate
52 Evaded the seeker
53 "Hail!" to Caesar
54 ___ Monte (food giant)
55 Prior, to Prior

ACROSS

1 Grounds for grounding?
5 Ghana's capital
10 Generation-spanning story
14 ___ as we speak
15 "They Died With ___ Boots On"
16 Gas station adjunct, often
17 Infamous Roman fiddler
18 Sixteen drams
19 Colored part of the eye
20 Concluding a sketch?
23 Reporter's badge word
24 Meddlesome woman
25 Passed (away), as time
28 Indefinite large number
30 Overseas currency unit
31 Garlic-flavored mayonnaise
33 Exxon offering
36 Like traffic approaching construction
40 Shade of summer?
41 Wind-borne silt deposit
42 Stick in the supermarket
43 White-sale purchases
44 Least honorable
46 Open spaces in malls
49 In unison
51 Losing steam
57 Not prerecorded
58 Informal "byes"
59 Stork relative
60 Break the seal on
61 Like Pisa's most famous landmark

62 Mountain lion
63 Hoses down
64 Hawaiian geese
65 Word with "movie" or "shooting"

DOWN

1 Fax or FedEx
2 Say with certainty
3 Transfusion fluids
4 January road clearer
5 Initiated repentance
6 Locomotive sounds
7 Parts of dollars
8 Puerto ___
9 Math student's calculation, sometimes
10 "I'm just kidding!" emoticon
11 Moses's older brother
12 Mill fodder
13 On the ocean or in a fog
21 Anger
22 Skeptical sort
25 Wagon train's direction
26 Dance to a ukulele
27 Branding rod
28 Cows' chorus
29 Words after "chicken" and before "king"
31 Has birthdays
32 It is in most dialogue?
33 Mighty wind
34 Leaves speechless
35 Part of an armed bandit
37 Trojan War epic

38 Wordless "yes"
39 Flowery vitamin C sources
43 Sheets, tablecloths, etc.
44 Lifts, as morale
45 Santa ___ (city in California)
46 Softly lit
47 Third-rate writing
48 Heavy metal fastener
49 "Won't Get Fooled ___"
    (The Who tune)

50 Took illegally
52 "Not if ___ help it!"
53 Evening, in advertising
54 Touch the border of
55 Bean variety
56 Former absolute ruler

ACROSS

1 ___ serif (type style)
5 Prime invitees
10 Matinee follower?
14 Malarial symptom
15 Vision-improving device
16 Actress Campbell
17 Suburbanite's fundraiser
19 Not loose-fitting
20 Bride's path
21 Master thespians they're not
22 Contents of some barrels
23 Villainous expressions
25 Gambler's milieu
27 FBI employee
29 Bench-clearing incident
32 Young bucks
35 Loose overcoat
39 Center of activity
40 Santa ___ winds
41 Not give up
42 Phoenix-to-Philly dir.
43 Motor lodge
44 Make a formal retraction
45 Low, sturdy cart
46 Chocolate bean
48 About 2.2 lbs
50 Credits follow it
54 Dig with the snout (Var.)
58 Sickly, as a complexion
60 Pasture chorus
62 Plait
63 Attack, cat-style
64 One place to relax

66 Dance done in grass skirts
67 Occur as a result
68 1958 Pulitzer winner James
69 Slippery and slithery
70 It's on the Aire
71 View from 64-Across

DOWN

1 Stories that span generations
2 Time and ___
3 Person with a bedside manner
4 Sailor's bearings
5 Tavern order
6 Flirtatious batter?
7 Asimov or Newton
8 Town of a civil rights march
9 Rapunzel feature
10 Non compos mentis
11 Certain scout leader
12 Egg, to a biologist
13 Brand of building blocks
18 Antibiotic target
24 Rani's garment (Var.)
26 Does not exist
28 Cop who might go undercover
30 Bluefin, for one
31 Old wedding vow word
32 Secular
33 Noted tutor in Siam
34 Big band venue
36 Group overseeing U.S. property
37 Chain piece
38 Showing signs of life

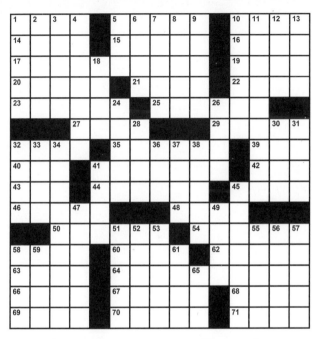

41 Propel, as into action
45 Threshold
47 "Be that as it may ..."
49 T-ball pitches
51 See 41-Down
52 "___ will ever guess!"
53 Wasteland shrub
55 Evergreen forest of subarctic lands
56 Luxury ship

57 Double-___ sword
58 Tooth or tummy problem
59 Swing around, nautically
61 Kind of ballistic missile
65 "For ___ a jolly good ..."

solutions

SOLUTIONS

1

S	L	A	S	H		E	D	W	I	N		B	A	M
A	O	R	T	A		T	I	A	R	A		A	G	O
G	R	E	A	T	S	H	A	K	E	S		L	I	T
S	E	A	B	R	E	E	Z	E		C	A	L	L	I
			B	E	E	R		B	E	L	I	E	F	
B	I	P	E	D	S		H	A	I	N	E	S		
A	M	A	D		H	A	V	O	C		T	A	M	
S	S	W		W	A	Y	J	O	S	E		I	L	O
S	O	N		A	D	M	I	N		S	C	U	M	
	B	A	R	O	N	S		S	P	A	S	M	S	
W	O	R	L	D	S		B	E	E	N				
R	I	O	T	S		B	O	A	R	D	G	A	M	E
I	L	K		H	O	L	D	S	B	A	R	R	E	D
T	E	E		I	N	U	I	T		N	I	C	A	D
E	R	R		P	E	E	N	S		T	A	S	T	Y

2

B	A	S	S		A	J	O	K	E		A	N	E	W
A	S	I	A		L	E	P	E	R		P	E	R	E
T	H	E	S	U	L	T	A	N	O	F	S	W	A	T
T	I	N	S	M	I	T	H	S		L	I	S		
E	E	N		P	S	A		M	U	S	T	E	R	
D	R	A	Y			S	P	R	A	T		Y	E	A
			E	O	N		A	E	R	I	A	L	L	Y
H	I	T	S	A	N	D	M	I	S	S	E	S		
R	E	M	I	T	T	E	R		N	T	H			
A	R	P		M	E	T	E	S			E	A	T	
D	A	L	L	A	S			C	H	I				
O	A	R			R	A	T	C	H	E	T	E	D	
S	T	R	I	K	E	U	P	T	H	E	B	A	N	D
E	W	E	R		I	S	L	E		O	N	C	E	
T	O	S	S		K	N	E	E	S		N	E	E	D

3

L	E	O		S	A	U	N	A		M	U	S	T	
O	A	R	S		A	C	T	O	N		U	N	T	O
G	U	I	T	A	R	H	E	R	O		F	L	U	E
		F	O	X	I	E	R		P	A	T	E	N	
A	L	I	C	E		S	I	C	I	L	I	A	N	S
C	A	C	K	L	E		H	A	T		R	E	P	
T	H	E	A		M	A	L	L		H	A	N	D	Y
			D	R	U	M	S	O	L	O	S			
C	A	M	E	O		I	D	E	A		B	E	A	D
O	N	O		U	R	N		C	H	E	A	T	S	
S	N	O	O	T	I	E	S	T		A	S	C	O	T
	U	N	P	E	G		H	E	A	L	T	H		
O	L	L	A		H	O	R	N	B	L	O	W	E	R
W	A	I	L		T	H	E	S	E		S	A	G	A
A	R	T	S		S	O	W	E	D			Y	O	N

4

R	A	N	G		S	W	A	B		H	O	S	P	S
O	L	I	O		T	R	U	E		O	P	T	I	C
C	O	N	S		I	O	T	A		O	S	A	K	A
K	E	E	P	I	N	T	O	U	C	H		Y	E	N
			E	D	G	E		H	A	R	A	S	S	
L	I	S	L	E			H	E	E	H	A	W		
A	R	E		A	E	R	A	T	E		S	H	I	T
V	O	T	E		V	E	N	U	S		P	I	S	H
A	N	T	E		E	D	D	I	E	D		L	E	A
	L	L	A	N	O	S			I	N	E	R	T	
C	R	E	S	T	S			S	A	N	E			
L	A	D		H	O	L	D	T	H	E	L	I	N	E
A	D	O	B	E		E	R	I	E		S	O	O	T
R	O	W	A	N		G	A	L	A		O	W	E	N
A	N	N	A	S		O	W	E	D		N	A	S	A

113

SOLUTIONS

5

Across/Down filled grid:

```
A U T O   B E L A Y   S M E W
G R O W   A G I L E   M A Y A
A B U N C H O F B A L O N E Y
V A R S I T I E S     I T D
E N E   A S S   O B E R O N
S E R B   M I N C E   A B A
A B E   D E E R S K I N
S M A L L P O T A T O E S
S E A L E V E L   N Y C
A C T   M E N S A   K A R T
T S U R I S   T O T   P E E
R E S   A B O R I G I N E
P E A C H E S A N D C R E A M
I N T O   D E I C E   A C M E
E D E N   O A T E R   N E E D
```

6

```
H E M   H O L D S   A R C O
A R A B   A B O U T   W E I R
W A L L F L O W E R   F A T E
L O I T E R   O C U L I
G N A W S   S Y M B O L I Z E
N O R T H   Y E R   G E L
U R D U   P O R T   N A N N Y
B R A N C H O U T
R O D E O   S A S H   T R A P
E T A   A B E   S L E U T H
B A S E M E T A L   I S L E D
L H A S A   D I L A T E
E G O S   G R A S S R O O T S
L I F T   L O T T A   R U E R
O A F S   E G E S T   T A I
```

7

```
A T L A S   S P U D   D R A T
N A I R A   W O K E   R A V E
E X E A T   A L A S   E D E N
W I N B Y A N O S E   A I R S
S R I   E R E M I T E
O A K   S K E W   T A T
S N I P   E X I T   R E S I N
L O S E O N E S B A L A N C E
O N S E T   S E A R   M O B S
R I M   D R E W   G M T
R I N G S U P   N O S
O D O R   D R A W A B L A N K
L E V O   P I L E   B A C O N
E S A U   I C O N   L I E G E
S T E P   E K E D   E N D O W
```

8

```
C O W L S   G O O F S   A R C
A W A I T   E X A C T   B A H
B E G F O R M E R C Y   R N A
T R A I N S   L A G S
V I T A M I N   I B I D E M
A R A B   L I F E S A V E R
T I L L S   E L M S
S E E K A D M I S S I O N
E X A M   I N K E D
I N T E L L E C T   T R A Y
O P I A T E   R O S E A T E
K E N T   S E A D O G
A C E   P R A Y F O R R A I N
P A T   E C L A T   E A G L E
I C Y   P A T S Y   S L A K E
```

9

S	P	I	N	A	L		A	C	E		C	O	M	A
U	R	S	I	N	E		G	A	Y		O	M	A	N
F	A	L	L	I	N	L	O	V	E		V	E	R	A
F	I	E		S	I	E	G	E		R	E	L	I	T
E	S	T		E	N	S		I	R	E		E	G	O
R	E	S	T			S	U	N	U	P		T	O	M
		I	N	S	E	T		N	E	A	T	L	Y	
	B	E	C	O	M	E	E	N	G	A	G	E	D	
C	U	C	K	O	O		R	A	S	T	A			
H	R	S		S	C	R	I	P		R	E	A	L	
A	N	T		E	K	E		A	C	T		A	P	E
T	S	A	R	S		F	E	L	L	A		T	I	N
T	I	T	O		G	E	T	M	A	R	R	I	E	D
E	D	I	T		O	R	C		U	S	A	N	C	E
L	E	E	C	H		A	S	H		S	I	N	G	E	R

10

P	R	A	Y		A	M	O	S		M	A	M	A	S
R	I	L	E		M	O	V	E		I	N	A	N	E
O	B	I	T		B	L	A	T		K	I	N	D	A
M	O	B	I	L	E	A	L	A	B	A	M	A		
P	S	I		E	R	R		A	D	A	G	I	O	
T	E	S	L	A		A	L	S	O			E	T	H
			A	S	S	U	M	E	S		O	R	S	O
		B	O	T	T	L	E	N	E	C	K	S		
E	W	E	S		O	N	E	S	T	A	R			
G	A	R		A	L	A	R			L	A	T	C	H
G	R	I	P	P	E		S	K	I		A	H	A	
		B	L	A	N	K	E	T	O	F	S	N	O	W
P	L	E	A	T		E	L	U	L		E	G	O	S
E	A	R	T	H		E	L	B	A		E	L	S	E
N	O	I	S	Y		L	A	S	S		P	E	E	R

11

E	L	K		B	A	A		N	I	P		B	B	C
N	O	N		A	C	T	U	A	R	Y		A	R	E
G	R	E	E	N	H	O	R	N	E	T		N	O	M
R	E	E	D		E	N	D		H	E	D	G	E	
A	L	L	O	W		C	U	S	T	O	D	I	A	N
F	E	E		E	W	E		T	A	N	G	E	N	T
T	I	D	I	E	R		F	I	X		I	D	S	
			S	P	I	D	E	R	M	A	N			
A	S	S		T	A	N		E	G	G	C	U	P	
A	C	C	U	S	E	R		A	N	A		A	L	E
F	R	E	E	P	R	E	S	S		R	E	R	U	N
G	E	N	R	E		O	P	T		G	A	L	A	
H	A	T		W	O	N	D	E	R	W	O	M	A	N
A	G	E		E	L	E	A	N	O	R		E	T	C
N	E	D		D	D	T		S	T	Y		L	E	E

12

G	A	D	S		C	A	P	O	S		G	A	G	A
O	P	E	C		A	R	O	S	E		P	L	A	N
S	P	A	R		R	E	N	A	L		O	K	R	A
S	A	F	E	C	R	A	C	K	E	R		A	L	L
I	L	L	E	R			E	A	C	H		L	A	O
P	L	Y		Y	A	M			T	O	K	I	N	G
			S	P	R	E	A	D			I	N	D	Y
		R	O	T	T	E	N	A	P	P	L	E		
A	S	E	A				T	Y	C	O	O	N		
C	O	R	P	S	E			E	E	L		M	B	A
A	B	E		A	L	T	O			I	C	I	L	Y
D	E	C		T	O	U	G	H	C	O	O	K	I	E
E	R	O	S		I	N	D	I	A		D	A	N	A
M	E	R	E			S	E	E	P	S		E	D	D	Y
E	D	D	A		E	R	N	S	T		D	O	S	E

115

SOLUTIONS

13

K	E	E	L		S	A	R	A	H		A	C	R	E
I	N	R	E		A	T	O	N	E		M	A	A	M
S	C	R	A	T	C	H	P	A	D		I	S	I	S
S	O	A		A	H	O	Y		G	A	G	E	S	
E	R	N		I	S	M		A	E	R	O	B	I	C
R	E	T	O	P		E	I	G	H	T		O	N	O
			L	E	I		S	A	O		S	O	S	O
	B	L	I	S	T	E	R	P	A	C	K			
A	S	E	A		L	E	E		S	P	A			
B	A	R		K	A	R	A	T		P	R	O	A	S
C	O	N	D	E	M	N		A	C	E		S	S	W
T	A	I	G	A		A	U	R	A		P	H	I	
H	O	R	A		B	U	M	P	E	R	C	R	O	P
M	M	D	L		A	R	I	E	S		P	E	R	E
M	E	S	S		D	I	D	S	T		A	Y	E	S

14

Z	A	N	Y		P	A	S	H	A		O	F	F	S
A	R	I	A		O	D	E	O	N		A	R	E	A
P	I	C	K	L	E	D	P	I	G	S	F	E	E	T
P	O	E	S	Y			T	S	E	T	S	E		
E	S	S		E	B	B		T	R	A		T	A	T
R	O	T	S		L	E	A		S	T	R	O	B	E
			A	B	O	A	R	D		I	O	W	A	N
	T	R	I	C	K	L	E	D	O	W	N			
B	R	A	G	G		S	E	C	O	N	D			
R	E	L	E	N	T		N	O	R		Y	A	L	E
A	M	I		A	H	S		R	Y	A		W	E	T
	S	E	M	I	T	E			L	E	A	S	H	
H	A	M	M	E	R	A	N	D	S	I	C	K	L	E
A	D	A	M		S	L	O	O	P		H	E	I	R
T	O	N	Y		T	E	S	T	Y		O	N	E	S

15

L	A	S	H		B	A	R	B	S		S	T	A	B
I	O	W	A		O	R	I	E	L		H	A	V	E
P	R	E	T	T	Y	U	G	L	Y		E	P	E	E
I	T	A	L	Y		M	I	L	L		K	E	R	F
D	A	T	E	R	S		D	A	Y	B	E	D		
			S	O	L	I		E	L	L	I	S		
P	E	G	S		E	N	A	B	L	E		I	R	E
E	D	O		P	E	N	G	U	I	N		V	O	W
E	G	O		I	T	S	E	L	F		M	E	N	S
P	E	D	R	O			B	E	T	A				
		G	U	N	N	E	R		R	U	L	E	R	S
O	A	R	S		O	P	A	L		R	E	L	I	T
F	R	I	T		H	O	M	E	O	F	F	I	C	E
F	E	E	L		I	C	I	E	R		I	S	I	N
S	A	F	E		T	H	E	R	E		C	A	N	T

16

C	H	A	P		A	L	O	H	A		M	I	S	E
H	O	N	E		L	A	P	U	P		I	M	P	S
A	O	N	E		S	I	E	G	E		S	P	O	T
S	H	O	R	T	O	R	D	E	R	C	O	O	K	
S	A	Y	S	O			R	C	A			L	A	G
E	S	S		N	I	G	H		U	R	S	I	N	E
			V	E	I	L	E	D		I	T	E	M	
	M	E	D	I	U	M	R	A	N	G	E			
F	A	N	G			E	P	I	G	O	N			
I	C	E	A	G	E		S	P	A	N		P	A	D
T	O	M		I	D	S			E	M	O	T	E	
L	O	N	G	I	N	T	H	E	T	O	O	T	H	
S	Y	N	E		T	O	W	E	L		C	L	I	O
O	T	I	S		O	R	I	E	L		H	E	R	R
S	E	C	T		R	E	N	D	S		A	D	E	N

SOLUTIONS

17

C B S		F A C T		M O U S E
A R T		A R R O W		I M P E L
S E E		R E C T I		S I S A L
C E A S E T O E X I S T
A D D I N		T O O		D U E
D E F R A U D S		N U D I S M
E R A		M O P E		R U S E S
S T O P W O R K I N G
O N T A P		N O N E		R A H
D I L U T E		L E G A L A G E
E L Y		I L K		B A C O N
C O M E S T O A N E N D
A A R O N		T H I N S		F I R
F L O R A		C I N C H		U Z I
T I D A L		H A T E		L E X

18

B I A S		C H A N T		D I C E
I N C H		R O G U E		I M P S
L U C Y		A R O M A		S P A T
B R U S H I N G B R I D E
O N S T A G E		M A L T S
S E E S		T E S		P I L O T
R I M		S K A		N E R O
A P E		D E N T I S T		D E W
S E N T		L A O		S R I
A R C H E T Y P E		O A S T
P E A R L		V O U C H E S
M O M E N T O F T O O T H
P A P A		D E A L T		C U R E
A B E T		N A I V E		C L A D
L A D Y		A R L E N		A D D S

19

D A K A R		R H O		C Y C L E
U T I L E		O A F		H I R A M
D O L L S		T I T		I N A N E
S P L I T S C R E E N		C A N
E A T		N O N S K I D
D I P S T I C K		N E E D
I T O		E L L E N		D R O P S
K E P T		T I R E S		A W O L
E M C E E		I N E P T		N P R
U N D O		S T R E S S E S
S O L D I E R		I A M
T N T		B R E A K G R O U N D
U S U A L		P U N		G O T O O
B E R N E		A T E		A C A S T
S T E T S		Y O W		S H H H H

20

O D D S		F E T U S		M A R
B E E N		I R A T E		B O N A
I N F A N T R I E S		I O N S
O R E		R A T T R A P
I L L E G		T I M A T E L Y
A N I		D A D O		E R E
I D A		S L A T S		A R C E D
D E N T		T H E M E		S H A D
E X T R A		O B E Y S		E R A
A L T		A L E C		E L Y
S W I M M I N G T R U N K S
P O M P A N O		L O B
O N E L		C H I L D P R O O F
K A T E		T O K Y O		A N N E
E T A		S W E E T		S E A N

117

SOLUTIONS

21

B	I	T	T	E		A	B	B	E		P	L	E	A
A	N	E	A	R		D	Y	A	D		R	E	A	R
O	N	E	F	R	O	M	T	H	E	H	E	A	R	T
B	A	T	T		V	I	E	T	N	A	M			
A	T	E		L	E	T	S		R	E	M	I	T	
B	E	R	B	E	R		A	R	T	D	E	C	O	
		R	A	L	E	I	G	H			S	E	W	
	T	W	O	F	O	R	T	H	E	R	O	A	D	
	H	U	E			R	O	T	A	T	O	R		
	E	N	N	E	A	D	S		O	M	E	L	E	T
M	E	T	A	L		P	A	R	A		A	N	O	
	S	O	P	R	A	N	I			A	N	D	S	
T	H	R	E	E	R	I	N	G	C	I	R	C	U	S
H	A	U	L		I	D	E	S		D	E	E	R	E
E	W	E	S		M	E	L	T		S	A	T	E	S

22

B	A	A	S		A	L	O	E		P	A	C	E	S
R	U	T	H		B	A	R	N		A	B	A	S	H
A	R	E	A		L	I	E	N		S	A	S	S	Y
C	O	O	K	I	E	D	O	U	G	H		T	E	N
T	R	U	E	D			I	M	A	G	I	N	E	
S	A	T		I	N	V	E	S	T		O	R	C	S
		W	O	O	E	R		I	N	T	O			
		B	U	T	T	E	R	P	E	C	A	N		
	S	C	A	R	S		O	A	R	E	D			
T	A	R	S		C	A	R	T	E	L		C	A	D
	U	N	I	T	A	R	D			L	O	U	S	E
P	O	T		F	U	D	G	E	R	I	P	P	L	E
O	N	O	U	R		I	N	T	O		A	T	O	P
R	I	N	S	E		C	A	N	E		R	I	P	E
S	C	E	N	E		T	W	A	S		T	E	E	N

23

G	R	A	T	A		S	K	I	S		R	U	B	
Y	A	R	E	R		E	I	R	E		S	I	N	E
P	R	I	C	E	I	N	D	E	X		A	N	N	A
S	I	S		A	C	I	D		T	A	G	G	E	R
U	T	E	N	S	I	L		A	B	A	T	E	D	
M	Y	N	A		L	E	E	A	N	N		O	D	E
		S	T	Y		A	N	T	E		N	E	D	
	A	F	A	R		B	V	D		R	E	E	D	
	O	N	O		A	C	R	E		L	S	D		
P	A	R		V	O	O	D	O	O		D	A	R	E
I	C	E	T	E	A		G	R	A	Y	S	O	N	
N	O	B	A	L	L		W	R	E	N		S	O	A
I	N	O	N		G	R	E	E	N	T	H	U	M	B
O	D	D	S		A	C	T	S		R	U	R	A	L
N	A	E		S	A	S	S		A	R	E	T	E	

24

T	O	G	A		B	O	W	E	D		D	A	M	P
A	R	I	L		E	R	O	D	E		E	M	I	R
B	A	L	I		H	I	R	A	M		S	O	M	E
U	L	T	E	R	I	O	R	M	O	T	I	V	E	S
			N	A	N	N	Y		U	S	E	R	S	
E	R	R	A	N	D			F	E	L	T			
M	E	A	T		B	E	A	M	S		V	I	E	
I	N	F	E	R	I	O	R	Q	U	A	L	I	T	Y
L	E	T		A	T	L	A	S		I	S	L	E	
		E	R	S	E		C	A	M	E	L	S		
A	B	O	V	E		T	I	A	R	A				
S	U	P	E	R	I	O	R	N	U	M	B	E	R	S
S	T	A	N		O	B	I	T	S		E	M	I	T
E	E	L	S		T	E	P	E	E		A	M	M	O
S	O	S	O		A	Y	E	R	S		N	A	S	A

SOLUTIONS

25

L	A	S	S	O		A	L	T	O		P	U	C	E
U	L	C	E	R		D	O	O	R		A	G	H	A
N	E	A	T	A	S	A	P	I	N		S	L	I	T
D	E	D	U	C	T		E	L	A	S	T	I	C	S

LASSO · ALTO · PUCE
ULCER · DOOR · AGHA
NEATASAPIN · SLIT
DEDUCT · ELASTICS
PLEA · STAR
WAR · ERRS · ELICIT
ADE · NITS · MEADE
CLEANASAWHISTLE
KIDDO · EPEE · EEN
OBSESS · HART · RDS
LEAD · TOUT
TREADLES · IBIDEM
SARI · IMMACULATE
ARID · NOUN · LEMUR
RENE · ANTI · ERNIE

26

RETORT · ROAR · CAT
NEARER · URGE · ADO
ALBINO · SCUD · RAT
SETSTHESTAGE
SOLO · PSI · ITEM
THINNER · DRAB
EAT · ASIA · ALICIA
TREADSTHEBOARDS
SERBIA · AKIN · ALI
BRYN · IDEATED
OIIO · YON · SERE
DIMTHELIGHTS
DNA · IRON · USURER
EGG · LINK · NAMELY
ROE · LESS · TREBLE

27

MUSCAT · ALAS · DIS
UNTRUE · NOCHARGE
SHIITE · NONUNION
TEL · INDEPENDENT
ERE · SIN · SOT
ROT · MEA · SIDETWO
SITE · HEIST
COMPLIMENTARY
IRONS · LEES
REGROWN · EST · PAT
EVE · CPA · ERR
SITTINGROOM · ANI
INSANELY · ITALIA
SCOTFREE · LAMENT
TEN · ODES · SMIDGE

28

GATE · MAMAS · TRAP
USED · ERICA · NOTE
SHAG · NINON · TUFT
HOPEFULSIGN · SIT
ERODE · KNEE · SRI
RET · RYA · RECESS
EMENDS · OATH
SKIPTOMYLOU
SLOE · ZOOMIN
TUNDRA · GAL · SHU
EGO · ALIA · AGUES
EGG · JUMPERCABLE
PARA · MEETA · EDEN
EGAD · NAACP · LUNE
DEMO · ANKHS · SEAT

SOLUTIONS

29

T	T	L		A	S	S		R	D	A		A	H	L
O	H	O		H	E	I	N	O	U	S		N	O	I
C	R	O	S	S	C	Z	E	C	H	S		T	R	A
C	O	T	E		T	E	A		O	C	E	A	N	
A	W	I	N	G		U	T	T	E	R	A	N	C	E
T	I	N		U	M	P		A	T	T	U	N	E	S
A	N	G	O	R	A		H	U	H		L	A	S	
		S	U	I	T	E	T	A	L	K				
P	U	B		D	U	D		N	E	S	T	E	D	
P	I	N	O	L	E	S		P	E	G		O	R	E
U	N	W	R	I	N	K	L	E		S	T	R	U	M
E	K	I	N	G		E	S	T		H	O	P	E	
B	I	N		H	O	R	S	E	S	C	E	N	T	S
L	S	D		T	W	O	S	T	A	R		T	E	N
O	H	S		S	E	T		A	R	T		O	D	E

30

L	I	C	H	I		C	O	P	Y		R	P	M	S
A	L	O	E	S		A	S	N	O		E	R	I	E
D	O	N	A	L	D	D	U	C	K		S	O	N	E
		F	L	A	R	E		E	D	I	S	O	N	
E	G	O		M	Y	T	H	O	L	O	G	I	S	T
L	O	U	T		S	A	L		I	N	T	O	O	
M	O	N	A	C	O		N	E	O	N				
		D	R	A	F	T	D	O	D	G	E	R		
U	F	O	S			E	S	T	A	T	E			
A	S	H	E	S		S	U	B		A	D	O	S	
S	T	O	M	A	C	H	P	U	M	P		I	T	S
C	U	P	O	L	A			R	E	L	I	C		
E	D	I	T		D	O	U	B	L	E	D	A	T	E
N	I	N	E		I	W	H	O		B	E	L	I	E
T	O	G	S		Z	E	S	T		E	A	S	E	L

31

G	A	L	A		S	H	A	L	E		S	A	G	A
A	R	I	L		H	A	R	E	S		A	P	E	X
M	E	N	D	F	E	N	C	E	S		L	O	N	E
E	N	G	E	L		S	E	R	E		A	L	E	S
S	T	O	N	E	D		D	Y	N	A	M	O		
			T	A	R	O		R	I	G	I	D		
C	A	S	E		I	N	S	I	T	U		I	T	E
L	E	U		D	E	C	O	R	U	M		Z	I	P
E	R	R		A	R	E	T	E	S		V	E	S	T
W	O	R	S	T			S	K	Y	E				
		E	N	A	M	E	L		S	U	T	U	R	E
A	C	N	E		I	L	I	A		R	E	V	E	L
B	O	D	E		C	A	L	L	A	T	R	U	C	E
C	H	E	Z		A	T	L	A	S		A	L	A	N
S	O	R	E			S	E	E	R	S		N	A	P	A

32

C	R	O	W		S	H	O	R	N		A	B	E	T
H	E	B	E		P	O	L	I	O		S	A	G	A
O	P	E	N	P	A	N	D	O	R	A	S	B	O	X
L	A	Y	T	O	R	E	S	T		M	A	Y		
L	I	E		E	S	S		T	A	M	T	A	M	
A	D	D	S		T	E	N	E	T		A	G	A	
			E	S	P		A	U	R	E	O	L	E	S
		B	A	T	H	I	N	G	T	R	U	N	K	S
S	U	M	T	O	T	A	L		A	R	T			
O	R	B		T	A	P	E	R		O	A	F	S	
T	R	U	M	P	S		E	R	A			B	U	M
		L	O	U		C	I	G	A	R	I	L	L	O
Q	U	A	R	T	E	R	B	A	C	K	S	A	C	K
I	S	N	T		V	O	I	L	E		L	U	R	E
D	O	T	S		A	P	S	E	S		E	T	A	S

120

SOLUTIONS

33

W	E	'/R	E		E	P	S	O	M		N	A	I	F
I	M	A	M		S	A	C	R	A		E	D	D	O
D	O	G	B	I	S	C	U	I	T		G	O	E	R
T	R	E	A	D		T	R	E	E		A	G	E	D
H	Y	S	S	O	P		F	L	O	A	T	S		
			S	L	A	P		W	E	L	S	H		
G	U	I	T	A	R					I	C	E		
O	N	O		L	E	P	R	O	S	Y		F	A	A
B	O	G			A	S	S	E	N	T		T	E	R
E	N	E	M	Y			K	I	T	E				
		A	I	S	L	E	S		R	U	A	N	D	A
A	R	T	S		E	G	O	S		P	L	A	I	N
B	O	D	E		P	R	A	I	R	I	E	D	O	G
B	O	O	R		T	E	R	R	Y		A	I	D	S
E	D	G	Y		A	T	S	E	A		F	R	E	T

34

A	D	D		P	A	S	T	E		B	A	B	E	L
G	E	E		E	T	H	E	R		A	B	O	V	E
A	N	N		W	H	I	R	S		S	L	U	E	D
V	O	I	C	E	O	F	R	E	A	S	O	N		
E	V	E	R	E	S	T		N	O	O	D	L	E	
S	O	R	E			I	P	S			M	A	I	L
			E	N	D		N	E	W	T		R	E	M
		S	P	E	A	K	F	R	E	E	L	Y		
A	S	H		E	M	I	R		R	A	E			
B	I	O	S		A	D	A	R		A	L	A	S	
C	R	O	C	U	S			E	C	O	N	O	M	Y
		T	A	L	K	O	U	T	O	F	T	U	R	N
B	R	O	N	C		P	L	A	N	T		S	I	T
A	C	U	T	E		U	N	I	T	E		E	T	A
S	A	T	Y	R		S	A	N	E	R		S	A	X

35

R	A	G	E		P	L	A	C	E		A	M	O	K
I	D	E	S		L	A	V	A	S		Z	U	L	U
D	O	N	K	E	Y	C	A	R	T		A	L	A	R
G	R	O	I	N		K	I	L	O		L	E	F	T
E	N	A	M	O	R		L	A	P	P	E	T		
			O	L	I	O		R	A	R	E	R		
A	R	C	S		G	R	O	T	T	O		A	T	E
C	I	A		R	H	E	N	I	U	M		I	N	S
T	O	M		I	T	S	E	L	F		S	N	A	P
		S	T	E	R	N		E	T	A	L			
		L	E	G	A	T	E		S	M	I	T	H	S
A	A	H	S		G	H	E	E		I	D	E	A	L
B	N	A	I		H	O	R	S	E	S	E	N	S	E
A	K	I	N		A	R	I	S	E		R	E	T	E
T	A	R	S		S	N	E	E	R		S	T	E	P

36

C	A	T		I	D	A	H	O		S	H	O	V	E
A	S	H		S	E	R	U	M		L	I	R	A	S
C	I	R	C	L	E	T	H	E	W	A	G	O	N	S
K	N	O	W	E	R	S		L	I	G	H	T		
L	I	N	T	S		H	E	N		L	U	T	E	
E	N	E		B	E	A	T			C	A	N	O	E
R	E	S	T		I	L	L		S	E	N	D	E	R
			O	V	A	L	F	A	C	E	D			
L	L	A	M	A	S		W	H	O		S	A	P	S
E	A	R	L	S		M	I	S	T			M	A	T
G	O	B	I		G	O	T			O	H	A	R	E
		I	N	C	A	S		N	A	N	E	T	T	E
E	A	T	S	A	S	Q	U	A	R	E	M	E	A	L
F	R	E	O	N		U	N	P	I	N		U	K	E
T	E	R	N	E		E	A	S	E	D		R	E	D

121

37

38

39

40

41

C	E	L	I	A		T	E	M	P	O		S	H	U
A	R	E	N	T		A	F	O	R	E		T	E	N
P	I	N	C	H	H	I	T	T	E	R		E	N	D
E	N	S	I	L	E		S	E	C		C	A	N	E
			S	E	W	S		T	I	T	U	L	A	R
A	P	P	E	T	I	T	E		S	A	T	A		
M	O	O		E	N	I	D		B	I	K	E	R	
I	R	A	Q		G	R	U	B	S		N	I	P	A
R	E	C	U	R		C	O	O	P		S	E	T	
H	I	E	S		E	G	R	E	S	S	E	S		
F	R	E	T	F	U	L		S	T	O	P			
L	O	D	E		P	I	A		O	N	E	I	D	A
A	B	E		L	I	F	T	A	F	I	N	G	E	R
R	I	G		A	N	E	E	D		E	C	O	L	E
E	N	G		P	E	R	E	Z		S	E	R	E	S

42

C	H	E	C	K		B	A	C	K		L	E	A	P
R	E	P	R	O		A	L	A	N		E	T	N	A
T	R	E	A	D		N	I	C	E		M	U	O	N
B	E	S	I	D	E	T	H	E	P	O	I	N	T	
			S	A	O			E	L	A	N			
R	O	C		K	L	A	N		S	N	A	T	C	H
E	B	O	N		E	N	O	S		I	D	A	H	O
B	E	H	I	N	D	T	H	E	S	C	E	N	E	S
E	L	E	N	A		I	O	T	A		S	K	A	T
C	I	N	E	M	A		W	A	C	K		S	P	A
			T	E	N	T			R	N	A			
I	N	S	I	D	E	S	T	R	A	I	G	H	T	
N	O	P	E		M	A	Y	O		F	R	E	O	N
T	R	O	T		I	R	K	S		E	E	R	I	E
O	A	T	H		A	S	E	A		D	E	A	L	T

43

S	C	A	R	P		T	A	G		G	A	P	E	D
C	O	M	E	R		E	R	R		I	R	E	N	E
A	M	O	C	O		L	E	A		T	E	A	S	E
B	A	K	E	D	A	L	A	S	K	A		C	U	D
			D	U	N			P	I	N	C	H	E	S
E	C	L	E	C	T	I	C		D	O	R	M		
M	O	I		T	I	T	H	E		S	I	E	G	E
I	R	M	A		S	E	E	M	S		B	L	U	R
R	E	E	V	E		M	A	I	N	S		B	R	A
			S	E	M	I		P	L	A	T	E	A	U	S
S	C	O	R	P	I	O			F	U	N			
T	A	R		R	I	C	E	P	U	D	D	I	N	G
I	M	B	U	E		E	R	E		D	E	F	O	E
L	E	E	K	S		A	S	S		E	A	S	E	L
T	O	T	E	S		N	E	T		D	R	O	S	S

44

E	T	C	H		R	I	L	L		B	A	M	B	I
L	I	R	A		E	T	U	I		A	D	O	R	N
F	L	A	S	H	B	A	C	K		L	O	T	U	S
			C	H	A	I		Y	E	P	S		L	I	E
A	S	K		I	D	A		N	E	A	R	E	S	T
S	A	P	O	R		M	U	S	T		E	Y	E	S
S	C	O	R	P	I	O	N		I	F	S			
	T	W	I	N	K	L	E	T	O	E	S			
E	N	D			I	T	E	R	A	T	E	D		
A	W	O	L		I	O	T	A		S	T	I	L	E
T	A	B	L	E	A	U		L	A	O		P	I	N
E	L	L		I	N	S	T		N	O	S	E		
A	L	O	U	D		T	R	I	C	K	K	N	E	E
S	E	N	S	E		E	A	V	E		A	D	E	N
E	D	G	A	R		R	Y	E	S		T	S	K	S

123

45

A	T	T	I	C		B	E	T	A		F	E	E	S
S	W	I	S	H		A	D	E	N		E	X	I	T
H	A	M	M	E	R	L	O	C	K		D	E	L	E
		E	S	S	E	S		H	O	O	T	E	R	
C	A	B		S	M	A	L	L	S	C	R	E	E	N
S	T	O	P		M	O	O		E	A	R	N	S	
I	A	M	S	A	M		T	O	I	L				
		B	U	L	L	E	T	P	R	O	O	F		
M	I	M	E		A	T	T	E	S	T				
F	A	R	G	O		M	R	S		B	A	K	E	
O	V	E	R	S	T	A	Y	I	N	G		R	I	D
C	A	P	I	T	A		R	E	A	P	S			
S	T	A	N		B	A	R	R	E	L	R	O	L	L
L	A	I	D		O	G	E	E		A	I	M	T	O
E	R	R	S		R	O	D	E			S	E	E	D	Y

46

C	H	E	F		P	A	S	T	E		P	A	S	T
H	E	R	A		I	S	L	E	S		E	L	A	N
A	R	R	I	V	E	S	O	N	T	H	E	D	O	T
R	E	A	L	I	T	I	E	S		E	V	E		
T	O	T		P	A	S		C	L	E	R	G	Y	
S	N	A	P		I	D	E	A	L			M	A	E
		E	M	U		A	R	R	I	V	A	L	S	
B	R	E	A	K	I	N	G	P	O	I	N	T		
E	L	E	P	H	A	N	T		I	N	N			
S	I	P		A	S	K	E	W		E	A	S	T	
S	P	R	I	T	E		A	W	E		T	H	E	
		I	S	M		A	R	L	I	N	G	T	O	N
G	E	S	T	A	T	I	O	N	P	E	R	I	O	D
O	R	A	L		U	N	D	U	E		E	R	I	E
D	E	L	E		B	U	S	T	S		W	E	N	D

47

A	L	A	R		D	I	E	M		D	E	F	A	T
R	I	L	E		E	I	R	E		E	R	I	C	A
C	E	A	S	E	F	I	R	E		L	O	N	E	R
H	U	S	T	L	E		T	U	T	T	I			
			V	A	N	E		N	O	I	S	E	S	
S	K	E	L	E	T	O	N		R	I	C	H	L	Y
P	A	N	E	S		S	T	A	I	D		L	A	N
R	I	D	E		B	E	I	N	G		T	I	T	O
A	S	P		T	A	S	T	E		M	I	N	E	D
N	E	R	V	E	S		L	A	Z	I	N	E	S	S
G	R	O	I	N	S		E	R	I	N				
		D	O	N	O	R		P	U	D	D	L	E	
O	V	U	L	E		S	T	O	P	S	D	E	A	D
R	I	C	E	R		V	I	N	E		A	L	M	A
B	A	T	T	S		P	E	E	R		Y	L	E	M

48

M	A	M	M	A		L	O	P	E		T	H	A	N
O	N	A	I	R		E	B	O	N		H	A	L	E
D	O	W	N	A	N	D	O	U	T		E	L	S	E
E	N	R	O	B	E		E	L	E	V	A	T	O	R
			R	I	L	E			T	R	O	T		
G	A	M		A	S	A	D		S	I	R	I	U	S
U	S	E			O	S	I	S			L	I	S	S	E
I	H	A	V	E	N	T	G	O	T	A	C	L	U	E
S	E	T	A	E		S	I	L	O			I	R	K
E	N	S	U	R	E		T	A	P	S		P	P	S
			L	I	N	D		R	I	O	S			
W	I	S	T	E	R	I	A		C	U	E	S	T	A
A	N	T	I		A	C	R	O	S	S	T	O	W	N
S	C	A	N		G	E	E	D		E	T	H	I	C
H	A	N	G		E	R	S	E		D	O	O	N	E

45   46

47   48

SOLUTIONS

49

H	A	L	F		E	D	D	A		T	R	E	A	D
A	G	E	E		N	E	A	T		R	U	M	B	A
D	O	S	E		V	E	N	T		E	S	S	A	Y
J	U	S	T	F	O	R	K	I	C	K	S			
I	T	O		L	I	S		R	O	S	E	T	T	E
S	I	N	C	E		K	E	E	N		A	R	E	
		O	S	S	I	A		W	O	O	L	E	N	
	F	I	S	H	I	N	G	T	A	C	K	L	E	
D	A	C	T	Y	L		L	A	Y	E	R			
O	R	E		I	T	E	M		L	A	T	E	R	
H	O	S	P	I	C	E		P	A	L		A	L	A
	S	N	A	P	D	E	C	I	S	I	O	N		
N	A	I	A	D		E	C	R	U		E	P	I	C
A	I	O	L	I		E	V	E	R		P	E	S	O
P	L	U	M	E		S	I	D	E		T	I	E	R

50

V	E	I	N		L	U	T	E	S		U	P	T	O
A	L	M	A		O	P	E	R	A		T	E	R	N
C	U	M	I	N	T	H	R	O	T	H	E	R	Y	E
A	D	U	L	A	T	O	R	S			E	R	A	
T	E	N		G	E	L		P	A	I	N	T	S	
E	D	E	N		D	E	C	A	L		N	I	T	
		U	S	E		P	O	S	T	L	U	D	E	
	M	A	K	E	G	O	O	D	T	H	Y	M	E	
D	I	V	E	R	G	E	D		A	Y	E			
I	C	E		F	A	R	E	S		S	I	P	S	
S	A	M	B	A	R		A	B	A		M	U	M	
			A	U	G		P	A	L	A	T	A	B	L	E
F	A	R	M	E	R	I	N	T	H	E	D	I	L	L
C	L	I	P		O	C	T	E	T		A	B	E	T
C	L	A	Y		M	A	I	D	S		R	E	D	S

51

L	I	B	E	L		F	E	Z		A	T	M	S
A	L	A	M	O		L	A	O		S	O	A	R	S
H	O	T	P	O	T	A	T	O		C	R	E	S	S
			T	S	A	R	S		P	A	T			
B	E	S	I	E	G	E		A	R	R	A	N	G	E
U	N	P	E	N	S		T	R	I	L	L	I	O	N
T	A	O	S		V	A	G	U	E		T	O	E	
	C	U	T	T	H	E	M	U	S	T	A	R	D	
I	T	S		E	Y	E	I	S		L	A	M	B	
T	O	A	S	T	E	R	S		B	O	O	T	E	E
O	R	L	E	A	N	S		S	E	R	P	E	N	T
			R	N	A		G	L	E	B	E			
A	D	I	E	U		I	N	A	P	I	C	K	L	E
B	A	N	N	S		R	A	T		T	I	E	I	N
A	N	N	E			E	W	E		S	A	G	E	S

52

I	S	O	D	D		C	P	A		B	A	R	E
S	P	A	R	E		H	O	W		A	U	G	E	R
T	A	K	E	A	H	I	K	E		L	D	O	P	A
			A	D	A	T	E		J	A	G			
L	A	U	R	E	L	S		L	A	B	E	L	L	E
E	L	N	I	N	O		L	O	C	A	T	I	O	N
D	I	C	E		V	E	N	O	M			N	U	T
	M	A	R	C	H	I	N	G	B	A	N	D	S	
H	E	N		O	A	S	I	S		A	S	I	A	
I	N	N	E	R	M	A	N		T	U	T	E	E	S
S	T	Y	M	I	E	S		M	A	R	T	Y	R	S
			E	N	S		B	O	M	B	E			
A	L	E	R	T		H	I	T	P	A	R	A	D	E
B	U	R	G	H		I	R	E		N	E	V	E	R
O	G	R	E			D	D	T		A	D	E	L	E

53

S	A	S	S		A	C	C	R	A		S	A	G	A
E	V	E	N		T	H	E	I	R		M	A	R	T
N	E	R	O		O	U	N	C	E		I	R	I	S
D	R	A	W	I	N	G	T	O	A	C	L	O	S	E
			P	R	E	S	S			Y	E	N	T	A
W	H	I	L	E	D			M	A	N	Y			
E	U	R	O			A	I	O	L	I		G	A	S
S	L	O	W	I	N	G	T	O	A	C	R	A	W	L
T	A	N		L	O	E	S	S		O	L	E	O	
		L	I	D	S			B	A	S	E	S	T	
A	T	R	I	A		A	S	O	N	E				
G	R	I	N	D	I	N	G	T	O	A	H	A	L	T
L	I	V	E		C	I	A	O	S		I	B	I	S
O	P	E	N		A	T	I	L	T		P	U	M	A
W	E	T	S		N	E	N	E	S		S	T	A	R

54

S	A	N	S		A	L	I	S	T		I	D	O	L
A	G	U	E		L	A	S	E	R		N	E	V	E
G	A	R	A	G	E	S	A	L	E		S	N	U	G
A	I	S	L	E		H	A	M	S		A	M	M	O
S	N	E	E	R	S		C	A	S	I	N	O		
			G	M	A	N			S	E	T	T	O	
L	A	D	S		R	A	G	L	A	N		H	U	B
A	N	A		P	E	R	S	I	S	T		E	N	E
I	N	N		R	E	C	A	N	T		D	R	A	Y
C	A	C	A	O		K	I	L	O					
		E	N	D	I	N	G		R	O	O	T	L	E
A	S	H	Y		M	O	O	S		B	R	A	I	D
C	L	A	W		P	O	R	C	H	S	W	I	N	G
H	U	L	A		E	N	S	U	E		A	G	E	E
E	E	L	Y		L	E	E	D	S		Y	A	R	D